CAMBRIDGE LIBRARY COLLECTION

Books of enduring scholarly value

Printing and Publishing History

The interface between authors and their readers is a fascinating subject in its own right, revealing a great deal about social attitudes, technological progress, aesthetic values, fashionable interests, political positions, economic constraints, and individual personalities. This part of the Cambridge Library Collection reissues classic studies in the area of printing and publishing history that shed light on developments in typography and book design, printing and binding, the rise and fall of publishing houses and periodicals, and the roles of authors and illustrators. It documents the ebb and flow of the book trade supplying a wide range of customers with products from almanacs to novels, bibles to erotica, and poetry to statistics.

Bibliopegia

John Andrews Annett was the pseudonym of John Hannett, a printer and a pioneer in the study of modern and historical bookbinding methods. *Bibliopegia, or the Art of Bookbinding*, first published in 1835 and enlarged the following year, was frequently republished and revised, and remains an important work on the subject. The author claims that it is the first practical manual on bookbinding to be published in England, derived from his own professional expertise and from recent French works on the topic. He explains every aspect of the process, from the folding of the sheets of paper and sewing, to the final finishing. He also discusses the various tools and machines in use, and provides a glossary of technical terms. This book is still a very valuable one for bookbinders and conservators, providing information on dyes and chemicals used in the 1830s as well as sewing and binding techniques.

T0371301

Cambridge University Press has long been a pioneer in the reissuing of out-of-print titles from its own backlist, producing digital reprints of books that are still sought after by scholars and students but could not be reprinted economically using traditional technology. The Cambridge Library Collection extends this activity to a wider range of books which are still of importance to researchers and professionals, either for the source material they contain, or as landmarks in the history of their academic discipline.

Drawing from the world-renowned collections in the Cambridge University Library, and guided by the advice of experts in each subject area, Cambridge University Press is using state-of-the-art scanning machines in its own Printing House to capture the content of each book selected for inclusion. The files are processed to give a consistently clear, crisp image, and the books finished to the high quality standard for which the Press is recognised around the world. The latest print-on-demand technology ensures that the books will remain available indefinitely, and that orders for single or multiple copies can quickly be supplied.

The Cambridge Library Collection will bring back to life books of enduring scholarly value (including out-of-copyright works originally issued by other publishers) across a wide range of disciplines in the humanities and social sciences and in science and technology.

Bibliopegia

Or the Art of Bookbinding, in All Its Branches

John Hannett

CAMBRIDGE
UNIVERSITY PRESS

CAMBRIDGE UNIVERSITY PRESS

Cambridge, New York, Melbourne, Madrid, Cape Town, Singapore,
São Paolo, Delhi, Dubai, Tokyo, Mexico City

Published in the United States of America by Cambridge University Press, New York

www.cambridge.org
Information on this title: www.cambridge.org/9781108021449

This edition first published 1836
This digitally printed version 2010

ISBN 978-1-108-02144-9 Paperback

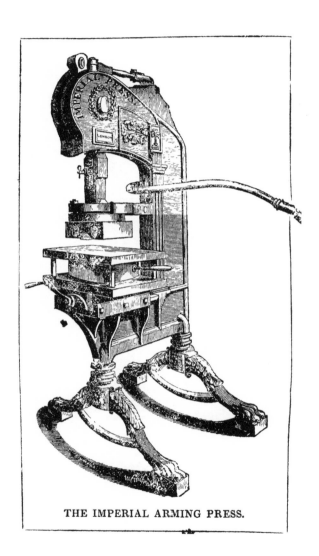

THE IMPERIAL ARMING PRESS.

BIBLIOPEGIA;

OR,

THE ART OF BOOKBINDING,

IN ALL ITS BRANCHES.

ILLUSTRATED WITH ENGRAVINGS.

BY JOHN ANDREWS ARNETT.

THE SECOND EDITION.
WITH CONSIDERABLE ADDITIONS.

LONDON:

RICHARD GROOMBRIDGE;

OLIVER AND BOYD, EDINBURGH; CURRY AND CO., DUBLIN;
AND W. JACKSON, NEW YORK.

1836.

G. H. Davidson, Printer,
Tudor Street, New Bridge Street, Blackfriars.

PREFACE.

THE following Treatise, in which will be found a variety of new, interesting, and valuable information, it is trusted, will supply a great desideratum ; no work relative to the Art of Bookbinding having been published in this country, that can be placed in the hands of the workman, calculated to assist him in the most important manipulations of his Art.

To render it of the greatest utility, the utmost care has been taken to give the most clear and comprehensive directions, in every department of the various processes required in binding a book, from the folding to the final operation ; and though some slight imperfections may have crept in, from the difficulty attendant on the investigation of a subject, respecting which little information could be derived from previous writers, it will be found that nothing has been omitted that could render the work as complete as possible. To this end, in addition to his own practical knowledge of the Art, the Author has availed himself of the communications of the best Workmen, and also of such parts of the productions of *M. Dudin, M. Lesne, M. Normand, M. Mairet*, &c., as experience has proved useful in practice.

Difference of opinion will doubtless arise as to the propriety of making known the more difficult operations of the

Art; but Science never lost by its general diffusion, and the clever workman will ever retain the elevated position which his taste, ingenuity, and attention entitle him to. With this view the work is submitted to the Trade, and public generally, as a miscellany of *real practical utility*, and a record of the present state of the BIBLIOPEGISTIC ART.

NOTE TO THE NEW EDITION.

Keeping pace with the inventions and improvements that have been introduced, it will be found that considerable additions and illustrative embellishment have been incorporated in the present edition. These, with a few emendations of parts above referred to, it is believed, now render the work as complete as it is at present possible to accomplish.

THE

ART OF BOOKBINDING.

INTRODUCTION.

In treating of the Art of Bookbinding as practised in the present day, it will not be necessary to enter into any discussion concerning either the antiquity of the Art, or the manner of preserving books, on and before the invention of printing, this being a subject requiring so much study and such extensive research, as to preclude its being brought within the limits of an introduction.

Binding is the art of folding the sheets of a book, securing them together, affixing boards or sides thereto, and covering the whole with leather or other materials. There are various styles of binding, as *half-binding*, where the backs and corners only are covered with leather, and the sides or boards with marbled or coloured paper. *Law binding*, which is generally confined to law books, the leather being left its natural colour, and the edges of the leaves plain. *Dutch binding* is where the backs are of vellum or parchment. *In boards* signifies that the book is slightly done up, and covered with paper or

cloth.   The styles of binding for the various classes
of literature are denominated by the titles of *filletted,
lettered, gilt, half-extra, extra, super extra*, according
to the quantity and style of work employed : thus we
say *calf, morocco*, or *russia extra*, &c.

The trade of a Bookbinder has been ranked among
the most difficult of the arts.   It is incontestibly one
requiring much care, great neatness, correct taste,
and attentive practice, to form a skilful workman,
and without these requisites no one will ever attain
the three great characteristics of good binding,—
solidity, elasticity, and elegance.   This will more
particularly be felt by the binder in small towns, who,
from his situation, cannot possess the advantages
which those of London, and other large cities, obtain.
The country binder has generally to exercise the
whole art, from the *folding* to the final operation
required in binding a book; whilst his more for-
tunate brother of the capital, from his business being
extensive enough to constantly employ *folders,
sewers, marblers, gilders,* &c. has himself to execute
what may be strictly called the binding only; viz.
the FORWARDING and FINISHING, and even these are
usually distinct branches.   The appearance of the
binding of a book, to a casual observer, seems to
require little talent, but if the various subdivisions of
the work, which form not less than sixty, are considered, and in the proper execution of which consists
the Art of Binding, it will not be surprising to find
how few men have arrived at eminence in it, arising

from the obstacles presented in the acquisition of excellence in every department. Difficult, however, as the whole routine may be to attain, and numerous as will be the discouragements on first trial of critical parts, yet with constant application and rigorous observations with regard to the various minor manipulations required, as well as the more important details, the attentive workman, whatever his situation, need not despair to reach perfection. To this end a clear and minute description of the various processes, in the order that they are employed in binding, will be given in the pages of this manual, uniting all that may be useful, not only to young and rising workmen, but to those considerably versed in the art. In the department of colouring leather, attention will be paid to present the best receipts, for though, according to the prevailing taste of the day, many of them are seldom used, still it is requisite that they should be known, as the fashion of another period may reintroduce the whole series of marbles and fancy colours ; and even now many periodical publications are required to be bound to patterns executed ten or twenty years ago. Some of the directions may, to the experienced, appear trivial or of no importance, but when it is considered that, by inattention to some part of the earlier stages of binding (such as being badly sewed, glued up, &c.,) the beauty of all subsequent operations is frequently destroyed, they must be pronounced *all-important* to the character of any one zealous of the reputation of a good binder.

The various errors and defects in the many important operations required in binding, will be pointed out under their respective heads; and a careful attention to the rules laid down will soon enable any individual, moderately expert, to execute binding worthy of a place in any library. Let it never be lost sight of that the proper *forwarding* a book is the great desideratum of all good bindings; the general appearance of the gilding and other ornamental operations being merely subservient to it. The early binders were rigid on this point, as is seen by their statutes and rules, edition 1750; and so particular were they that their books should be well forwarded, that the thirtieth article enacts,—" Be it held that the master-binders do sew all their books with thread and real bands, do back them with parchment and not paper, and in case of infringement the said books shall be done again at the expense of the infringer, who shall besides be condemned to a fine of thirty pounds for each volume." Solidity and elasticity are always found in the workmanship of the early binders, which has not been sufficiently observed by those of later times. Attention to these particulars has, however, of late been paid; and aided by superiority in material, and the machinery now employed, a degree of solidity and elasticity, combined with a lightness and elegance of appearance, has been attained, which the most approved bindings of the fifteenth century do not possess.

Care is of the utmost importance when the book is

valuable, either from its rarity, or the splendour of its embellishments, such works daily augmenting in price; for if carelessly or badly bound, the rebinding, and consequent *cropping* the book down by recutting the edges, tends considerably to deteriorate it in value, a good margin being a primary object to the genuine book collector. Many have contended that there is no occasion for this extra care in forwarding, since for a moderate sum other copies might be obtained, and thus the solidity and elasticity of the binding have been sacrificed to the general *coup-d'œil* of the finishing. Let not the binder, however, hazard his reputation on the effect thus produced, which will not be lasting, but rather let it be his ambition to produce such work as will bear the test of examination in every part, opening with freeness, and presenting an appearance at once firm, square, and compact. Should the possessor of a library limit his binder to price, he will do well also to sacrifice a portion of ornament (which adds nothing to the durability), to the charge necessary to be made for extra care in the earlier stages. Let him not be tempted by an elegant marble upon the cover and upon the edges, by a border full of delicacy and taste, by a gilding that pleases the eye, or by the gold spread with profusion upon the edges, the back, and the sides, to the neglect of the more important details of folding, sewing, cutting, &c. Rather let him not limit the binder too closely, and then, if he employs an experienced workman, he will be certain of receiving the satisfaction he desires, when presented with a volume possessing every characteristic of good binding. The knowledge communicated in this treatise, it is believed, will enable any one fully to appreciate superior workmanship, and once properly understood, none but the best will ever be satisfactory to the lover of his library. In the directions given, the amateur, who may take pleasure in devoting part of his leisure to an art interesting and amusing, will meet with all the information he may desire relative to the proceedings in use by the best binders.

The premises, presses, tools, and materials required by the bookbinder, are of much greater importance than, on first consideration, would be imagined. The great object in the former should be to procure as much light as possible, and with regard to presses, &c. unless they are of a superior kind, it will be impossible to execute binding in the first style of the art. These should be arranged with the greatest attention to convenience of situation, as much time will be saved from the facility with which the work will be executed, and from the additional neatness and beauty it will also acquire.

For the greater convenience of reference, and for properly distinguishing each branch of the art, a division into parts or sections has been deemed advisable. The technical terms will be found to have been adopted throughout; and though one volume only is generally spoken of, it must be observed that it is usual to proceed with parcels of ten, twenty, or more volumes at a time.

PART I.

OF FORWARDING.

As the gathering of the sheets of a book, after they have been printed and dried off, is nearly always performed at the printer's, it will not be necessary to enter into any details on that subject, but to consider as the commencement of binding, the operation of

FOLDING,

which is of great importance, the beauty of a book depending on its being properly and correctly folded, so that, when it is cut, the margin of the different pages may be uniform throughout, and present no transpositions, to the inconvenience of the reader and deterioration of the work.

The various sizes of books are denominated according to the number of leaves in which the sheet is folded ; as folio, quarto, octavo, 12mo, 16mo, 18mo, 24mo, 32mo, &c. Each form presents a certain number of pages, so disposed that, when the sheet is properly folded, they will follow the numeric order. In commencing the folding of any work, particular attention should be paid, in opening out the quires or sets, to observe that the *signatures* follow each other alphabetically, and, if consisting of two or more volumes, that the whole of the sheets belong to the right one.

Although each form is folded in a different manner, it will not be requisite to detail the whole, as a description of the octavo and twelvemo will amply furnish an idea of the proper way of folding the larger and smaller sizes.

Octavo.—The sheets being placed on the table with the signature, which will be seen at the bottom of the first page, turned towards the table at the corner nearest to the left hand of the workman, will present pages 2. 15. 14. 3. below, and above, with their heads reversed, pages 7. 10. 11. 6. (reading from left to right). The sheet is then taken with the left hand, by the angle to the right, and creased with the *folder* in the right hand, in the direction of the *points* made in the printing, taking care, by shading to the light, that the figures of the pages fall exactly one on the other, which will be 3 upon 2, and 6 upon 7, and thereby presenting uppermost pages 4 and 13, and above 5 and 12. The top part of the sheet is then brought down, with the left hand, upon the lower, pages 5 and 12 falling upon 4 and 13, directed properly, and again folded. The sheet then presents pages 8 and 9, which are then folded evenly, 9 upon 8, forming the third fold and finishing the sheet.

Twelvemo.—The signature to this size, when placed before the workman, should be at the top on his left hand, and towards the table, the sheet pre-

senting pages 2. 7. 11., 23. 18. 14., 22. 19. 15., 3. 6.
10. On the right, pages 11 14. 15. 10., are separated
from the others by a larger space, in the middle of
which are the points, indicating the proper place
where the ? pages should be cut off. The *Folder*
detaches this part, and placing page 11 upon 10 makes
a fold, and 13 upon 12, which will be uppermost,
finishes the folding of what is called the *inset*, and
which bears the signature of the sheet it has been
separated from, with the addition of a figure or
asterisk, as A 5, or A*. The remaining eight pages are
folded in the same way as the octavo, and when done
the inset is placed in the middle of it, taking care
that the head lines arrange properly.

Books are sometimes printed in what is called half
sheets, but they are folded the same, after cutting
them up; the octavo in the direction of the points,
the twelvemo in *oblong* direction of the paper, and
laying them apart from each other. There are also
oblong octavos, which are folded in the middle in a
line with the points, the second fold in the same
direction between the heads of the pages, and the
third on the length of the paper.

In the first fold of the octavo sheet is shown the
manner of folding the folio, and in the second the
quarto : the twelvemo also presents us with the
eighteens, after the sheet is cut into three divisions :
little or no difficulty will be experienced in folding any
other size that may occur, attention to the disposition
of the pages and signatures being only required.

It will often be found necessary to refold a book which, previous to being bound, may have been done up in boards, sewed, or otherwise. This should in all cases be carefully attended to, after the book has been taken to pieces, the back divested of the glue and thread, and the corners or other parts which may have been doubled, turned up. This is usually done by examining if the margin at the head and fore-edge is equal throughout, bringing those to their proper place that are too short, and cutting those that are longer than the general margin. By these means an uniformity will be presented after the edges of the book are cut, which could never be attained if not attended to whilst the book is in this state.

The sheets of the book being all folded, are gathered together, beat up between the hands on the table to bring them even, and then

COLLATED,

to see that the whole of the sheets belong to the same work and volume, as also that none are wanting. This is done by taking the book in the right hand by the upper corner of the fore-edge, and with the left, opening the sheets on the back and letting them fall successively one after the other. The signatures will be thus seen in alphabetical or arithmetical order, as A. B. C. &c., or 1. 2. 3. 4. &c., to the last, which should always be examined to ascertain that it is the completion of the book. By these means any sheet incorrectly folded is also detected. Books in folio and quarto are generally collated with a needle or pricker, by raising the sheets singly from the table, but this practice should be resorted to as little as possible, as the work is liable to be damaged. If any sheet is wanting or belongs to another volume, or is a duplicate, the further progress of the work must be suspended, till the imperfection is procured or exchanged. Those that have been wrong folded must be corrected, and any *cancels* occurring in the work, cut out, and replaced by the reprints which will generally be found in the last sheet of the book. It is usual also with some binders to place any plates belonging to the volume, at this period, but as the liability of damage to them is great in the process of *beating*, it will be much better to perform that operation after the book is brought from the stone, for which directions will be given. The book being found correct, will be ready for the beating-stone.

BEATING, PRESSING, &c.

The first operation is commenced by shaking the volume upon the stone by the back and head, so as to make the whole even, and facilitate the division of it into as many equal parts, which are called *sections* or *beatings*, as may be judged necessary according to the thickness and other circumstances. A section is then taken and well beaten over, drawing it with the hand towards the body so as to bring the various

c

parts successively under the hammer, and carefully avoiding striking more blows in one part than the other, except giving the edges a slight extra tap round. The section is then turned, and the like proceeding gone through; as also on each side after it has been separated, and the bottom part placed on the top, the middle of the section being thereby brought under the action of the hammer. This being done, the sheets are replaced in their proper order, and two or three taps with the hammer given to make them lay even. In beating those books with which, from their value, greater care is required, it is usual to place a guard or waste leaf of paper on each side of the section, to avoid any stains or marks which the stone or hammer might be liable to make.

It requires more skill than actual strength in beating, the weight of the hammer being nearly sufficient for many works. Attention must be paid to the hammer descending parallel to the surface of the stone, to avoid marking or cutting the sheets with the edge. Figure 3. plate v. shows the manner of holding the hammer, &c.

Before beating a book, care should be taken to observe if it has been recently printed, for if so it would *set off* by being beaten too much. This will be easily ascertained by referring to the date at the foot of the title or by smelling the ink it has been printed with, which, being composed partly of oil, will not have got perfectly dry. This will particularly be the case with machine printed works. As, however, it is frequently necessary to bind a volume immediately after being printed, it will be requisite to take every precaution against its setting off, which would destroy the beauty of the work It is the practice of some to put the book into an oven after the bread has been taken out, or into a stove heated sufficiently to dry the ink and make it search into the paper; but as these means are not without danger of getting the paper blackened or soiled, it is a better plan to interleave the sheets with white paper, which will receive all the ink set off. Should the sheets have been hotpressed, which is readily distinguished, this precaution will not be necessary.

When employed at the beating stone, the workman should keep his legs close together to avoid *hernia*, to which he is much exposed, if, with the intention of being more at ease, he contracts the habit of placing them apart.

A rolling press has lately, been invented as a substitute for the beating which books require previous to being bound. This will be fully described in the chapter on presses, where an engraved representation is given. Its operation is quicker and its power of compression greater, in a proportion of five sixths. A boy sits in front of the press and gathers the sheets into packets, by placing two, three, or more upon a tin plate of the same size, and covering them with another plate, the number of sheets depending on the stiffness and thickness of the paper. The packet is then passed between the rollers and re-

16

THE ART OF

ceived by the man who turns the winch, who has
time to lay the sheets on one side, and to hand over
the tin plates by the time that the boy has prepared
the second packet. These machines have been introduced into offices of great extent, and from the
economy of time and abridgment of labour, with the
best results; but it is a question whether they will
ever become general in those where the business is
limited, and their use but little called for.

After beating, should there be any plates to the
work, they, as before stated, must now be placed
among the text. Great care must be taken to make
the justification of the plates uniform with the text,
by cutting off any superfluity at the head or back,
and by placing them exactly facing the pages to which
they refer, pasting the edge next to the back. Any
that may be short at the head must be brought down,
to preserve an uniformity. It is advisable to place a
leaf of *tissue paper* before each plate, particularly
when newly printed, as the ink of copper-plates is
longer in drying than that of letter-press. When a
work contains a great number of plates, which are
directed to be placed at the end, they are sewn on the
bands by overcasting, which operation will shortly be
treated of in full.

The book being now ready for pressing, is taken
in sections, according to the work, and the judgment
of the workman, and placed between pressing boards,
the size of the volume, one on the other, and conveyed to the *standing-press*, which is pulled down as

tight as possible by the *press-pin*. To compress them the more, a *capstan* or winch is employed.

After the book has been sufficiently pressed, it will be necessary again to *collate* it, to correct any disarrangement that may have taken place during the beating and pressing.

SAWING THE BACKS.

This operation is performed to prevent the bands on which a book is sewn, appearing on the back. After beating the book up well on the back and head, it is placed between two *cutting boards,* the back projecting a little over the thick edge, and tightly screwed in the *laying* or *cutting press,* the whole being elevated sufficiently to prevent the saw damaging the cheeks of the press. Then with a *tenant saw* the proper number of grooves are made, in depth and width according to the diameter of the band intended to be used, which will depend on the size of the book. A slight cut must also be given above the first and under the last band, for lodging the *chain* or *kettle stitch.* It is very necessary that the saw should be held parallel with the press, without which precaution, the grooves being deeper on one side than the other, the work will present, when opened, a defect to the eye.

The *end papers,* which should consist of four leaves of blank paper, folded according to the size of the book, are now prepared and one placed at the beginning and end of each volume.

c 3

SEWING.

According to the number of *bands* wanted, must be attached to the loops on the cross-bar of the *sewing-press* (see figure 1, plate v.), as many pieces of cord, of proper length and thickness, and fastened with the aid of the *keys* in the groove of the press as nearly equal in tightness as possible. When this is done the back of the first sheet of the book is placed against the cords, which must be moved upwards or the contrary to the marks of the saw, when the small screws at each end under the cross-bar must be moved upwards till the strings are equally tight. All this being disposed, the book is commenced sewing by placing the end paper, which has no marks of the saw, on the sheet before laid down, and sewing it throughout, leaving a small end of thread to form the knot, after sewing the first sheet, which is then taken from under and sewn the whole length.

There are various ways of sewing, according to the size and thickness of the sheets of a book. A volume consisting of thick sheets, or a sheet containing a plate or map, should be sewn singly the whole length, in order to make the work more secure and solid. Great care should also be taken not to draw the thread too tight at the head or foot of the book, and to keep the back slightly swelled, the beauty of the binding depending much on this when the volume is backed.

When a book is sewed *two sheets on,* three bands

are generally used. Taking the sheet and fixing it on the bands, the needle is inserted in the mark made for the chain-stitch, and brought out by the first band; another sheet is then placed, and the needle introduced on the other side of the band, thus bringing the thread round it, sewn in like manner to the middle band, and continued to the third, when taking again the first sheet, it is sewn from the third band to the other chain-stitch, where it is fastened, and another course of two sheets commenced, and so continued to the last sheet but one, which is sewn the whole length, as directed for the first sheet, as also the end paper. Three bands are preferable to two, the book being more firm from being fastened in the middle, which is the only difference in sewing on two and three bands.

Half sheets, to obviate the swelling of the back too much, are usually sewn on four bands, which admit of three on a course: the first sheet is sewn as in three bands, from the chain to the first band, the next to the second, and the third takes the middle space; then the second sheet again from the third to the fourth band, and the first from thence to the other chain-stitch. The third sheet having only one stitch, it is necessary that, in sawing, the distance from the second to the third band should be left considerably longer than between the others. Quartos are generally sewn on five bands to make the work firmer, but if in half sheets, as in the folio size, six or more are used, sewing as many sheets on as bands, giving each sheet but one tack or sewing, and piercing the needle through the whole of the course at each end or chain-stitch before fastening the thread. This, which gives sufficient firmness, is necessary to prevent the swelling of the back, which a less number of sheets in a course would make, and spoil the appearance of the binding.

When the book is composed of single leaves, plates, or maps; or, as in the case of music, where, from the decayed state of the back, it is necessary to cut off a portion with the plough in the manner pointed out for cutting edges, the whole must be attached to the bands, by what is called *overcasting*. This is by taking a section, according to the thickness of the paper, and forcing the needle through the whole at the kettle-stitch, and on each side of all the bands, at a distance sufficient to secure the stitches from tearing, bringing the thread round each band as before directed, and fastening it at the end before proceeding with another course. To keep the whole of the sheets properly even, the back is sometimes glued immediately after cutting, and when dry divided into sections. Atlases and books of prints, when folded in the middle, will require a guard or slip of paper to be pasted to them so as to allow them to open flat, which they could not do if attached to the back, and which would destroy the engraving. These guards must be of strong paper, about an inch in breadth, and folded to the right size. They are sewn 'by overcasting, as above diiected.

The old mode of sewing on raised bands combines many advantages. This style is still adopted with many works, particularly those with limited margins. When the book is sewn on raised bands, it is only necessary to mark the place for the chain-stitch, and sew backwards over the cords to prevent the thread tearing the sheets, which it would if brought out on the near side of the bands. Folios and half-sheet quartos are generally sewn in this manner, in consequence of the inequality of the margins at the head, which are thus arranged properly by bringing the top line even with a band attached to the sewing-press as a guide. The defective parts are then removed when the book is cut.

It was proposed by *M. Lesne*, bookbinder of *Paris*, in a Memoir presented by him to the " *Societé d'Encouragement*," January 18, 1818, that in order to give to books the three essential qualities of binding, elasticity, solidity, and elegance, they should be sewn similar to the Dutch method, which is on slips of parchment, instead of packthread ; but to remedy the inconvenience arising from one slip being insufficient to make the back of a proper solidity, as well as being liable to break ; and if doubled or trebled, presenting a bad effect on the back when covered, he suggested the adoption of silk for the bands, which in a much less diameter is far stronger than packthread double the thickness. It is also preferable for sheets that require sewing the whole length, to use silk ; this being much stronger than thread, and insuring a greater solidity to the work.

The effects produced by the adoption of this style may be seen in the bindings of the finer class of Bibles, Prayers, &c. of the present day, which are sewn on very fine and strong cord with silk. It will be observed that the cuts of the saw, apparent in other bindings, are not seen in opening the volume; the bands form an ornament to the back, and each sheet revolves thereon as upon a hinge, the inner margin being preserved its full size, and the elasticity and freedom of the volume much increased.

When the volume is entirely sewn, the screws are loosened, the cords detached from the keys, and about two inches of the cord left on each side of the book to attach the boards that are to form the sides.

PASTING THE ENDS, GLUEING THE BACKS, &c.

The book being taken from the sewing-press, the two outside leaves of the end papers are pasted together to give additional strength to the joint when pasted down, and to hide any defects or stains in the boards, which, if single, would show through. When the volume is a folio or quarto, it is usual to paste the remaining two leaves in the same way, the largeness of their size requiring a greater consistency. But when the book is to be bound in an expensive manner, marbled or coloured ends must be pasted in. These are cut and folded in the same way as before directed, the coloured or marbled side being folded

inwards. The book is then placed before the workman with the fore-edge towards him; the first leaf
of the plain end paper is opened and laid back, and
one of the coloured ones placed about half over the
second, with the back or fold towards him; it is
pasted equally over, as well as the half of white not
covered, and then turned, fixed evenly and closely to
the back, and rubbed smartly to make it adhere.
The first leaf is then again brought over, and serves
as a guard until the coloured one is pasted to the
board. Attention should be paid, that such papers
only, as will blend well with the colour of the
leather intended for the cover, are used.

If a joint in calf or morocco is required, it should
always be uniform in colour with the cover, and
pared on the edges to reduce the thickness a trifle.
This joint should be about two inches broad, and
folded in the middle after being pared. It is pasted
on the white end paper on the side towards the
groove, the other part not being pasted to the board
till the book is covered. For additional strength
where the book is heavy, it is usual also to sew the
joint with strong silk to the bands.

These matters being adjusted, the whole end paper
must be turned from the back, the edge of the fold
slightly but evenly pasted with the finger, and
returned again, taking care to affix it close to the
back. The strings on which the book has been sewn
must be pulled tight, and a little from the back, so as
to avoid pressing on the end paper and bearing it off.

Some workmen do this previous to pasting the ends;
but from its being liable to tear near the bands and
chain-stitch, unless thoroughly dry, the mode of proceeding here described is much better.

The book is now taken between the hands and well
beaten up at the back and head on a smooth board,
to bring the sheets level and square, as the beauty of
the book in all the subsequent operations of binding,
depends on the care and attention paid in this place.
The volume is then held firmly by the fore-edge with
the left hand, the back, if not exceeding the width of
the front, swelled a little with the fingers of the right,
and glued equally over. Should it be a volume of
large dimensions, it will be necessary to place it
between boards, and put it lightly into the laying-
press, taking care that the sheets are even on the
back, and the volume equal in thickness throughout
the whole length. It is then laid on a board to dry,
but must not be placed before the fire, as by so doin
the sheets are liable to start from the back, and th
strength of the glue to be much diminished.

The back being dry, the bands on which it is sewn,
and which are intended to be laced in the boards,
must be opened with a bodkin and scraped with a dull
knife, so as to bring them to a point, and make them
more convenient to attach to the boards which are to
form the side covers.

BACKING.

In commencing this operation, which is done to form the groove for the reception of the boards, the book is placed upon the laying-press with the fore-edge towards the workman. The left hand should then be placed flat and open upon it, the thumb on the fore-edge; with the four fingers the leaves must be drawn forwards, and with the right hand, the back beat lightly on the edge with the *backing-hammer*, to give it a circular form. Both sides being thus *rounded*, one of the *backing-boards* is placed upon the volume at an equal distance from the back, according to the groove required for the board; then turning the volume, the other is placed in a similar manner, and the whole put carefully into the press, the lower edge of the boards even with the cheeks of the press, and screwed with the *press-pin* as tight as possible. With the hammer the back is then beaten firm and round, which causes the boards to form the groove on each side, by the projecting over of the part left above. Should the glue on the back have become too hard, or be too strong, it will be advisable before backing to damp it with a moist sponge. When the volumes are large, or plates attached to guards, the back, which bears the whole stress of the volume, should in every operation have all the strength given to it possible, and in the backing more particularly than any other.

D

BOARDING.

The milled boards used for covers being of various dimensions, similar to the sheets of paper, are cut according to the size of the book, in the same way as the end papers. The board is divided with the *compasses*, each part serving for one side of the cover. It is then marked in the direction of the points made by the compasses, with a bodkin and rule, and cut in the direction of the marks with the large *shears* fastened in the laying press. The side of the boards intended to be placed next the groove is then cut smooth in the press with the *plough*, and if intended for extra work, paper is generally pasted on one side, which gives the board an additional firmness. This part of the preparation should be done during the time the back of the book is drying, and previous to opening out the bands.

The boards lined with paper, as before directed, being dry, the volume is taken and one end of the compasses placed in the groove, and the other extended towards the fore-edge, to the extreme point the leaves will bear cutting, so as to present a firm and smooth edge. After allowing sufficient for the square of the board in front, the prepared boards must be marked at each end, and the rough part cut off with the plough in the same manner as previously done to the edge next the groove. One board is then placed on each side of the volume, even at the head, and marked with a bodkin opposite to the slips intended to be laced in ; a hole in a vertical position is then made through the board, and being turned, another in the same way near to the first. The bands having been pasted and passed in above, are returned through the other hole, and being pulled tight, the boards will necessarily be perpendicular to the back, and confined in the groove. After cutting off the ends of the strings near to the lace holes, they must be beaten well and evenly into the board, by placing the under part on an iron (called the *knocking-down iron*), fixed at the end of the laying-press, and beating above with the backing-hammer.

If it be desirable that the bands should not be seen inside, the hole may be made so vertical, that by placing the bodkin in the same on the other side, another verging a contrary way to the first may be made, and the band being passed in this one continued hole, will not be seen underneath. The liability, however, of its tearing out is an objection, and from this cause, the common way, with care in beating down, is preferable.

The volume is next placed between the pressing-boards, and put into the *standing*-press, which must be screwed tight and evenly down. The back is then damped with paste, and according to the firmness of the sewing and book, grated and scraped, and finally rubbed smooth with paper shavings, and left to dry in the press for as long a time as possible. If a large volume, it is usual to apply a little glue to the back.

When taken out of the press, the boards must be
disengaged from the end papers, where they adhere,
so that they may move freely up and down in the
cutting.

CUTTING THE EDGES.

The manner of preparing the volume for cutting is
very important, as a swerving from right angles in
cutting the head will present a disagreeable appearance, not only at the head but the tail also, which
being compassed from it, will display the same defect.
The top and bottom of the back should be at right
angles from the back, and the fore-edge parallel to it.
To perfectly insure this, it is better to use the *square*,
applying the edge to the front side of the board, and
marking the quantity necessary to be cut off at the
head, leaving all the margin possible. The boards of
the book are then drawn down, and the volume
placed, with the back towards the workman, on a
cutting board in the left hand ; the *runner* or smooth
edged board is then fixed on the other side, with the
right hand, even and square with the line above
directed to be made, and the whole held tight with
the left hand, put into the cutting-press, to the level
of the right hand cheek of the same, taking care that
the volume hangs perpendicular to the cheeks of the
press. Being screwed tight with the pin, the workman then takes the plough, with the right hand, by
the head of the screw, and placing it on the groove of

the press, proceeds to cut the book, holding the other end of the screw firmly with the left hand, and causing the knife to advance gradually through the book, by turning the screw gently as he cuts, which should be all one way, viz. as the arms are removed from the body. The plough must be held firm in the groove, or rods of the press, to prevent the knife jumping or cutting the edges uneven, and should the knife be found to run up or down, the defect must be remedied by removing some of the paper or boards placed under the knife where it is fastened to the plough. If there should be none required to bring the knife even with the plough, then a piece must be placed on whichever side of the *bolt* the defect may require.

The head being cut, the book is taken out of the press, and the quantity to be taken off the tail marked with the compasses. For this purpose the book is opened, and search made for the shortest leaf, which is measured by placing the thumb of the left hand against the edge of the head, and applying against it one of the points of the compasses, carrying the other so much over the end of this leaf, as will allow for the square of the boards at the head and tail. Then shutting the book, the distance is marked near the back and fore-edge on the board. To be more correct, a line may be marked from the two points made, and the square will detect any error that may have been made in cutting the head. The boards are then drawn equally over the head of the

book to the distance allowed for the squares, put into
the press, and cut at the tail.

Much precaution is necessary in cutting the fore-
edge. Mark the book with a bodkin on the projecting part of the end papers, and on each side, at
the head and foot close to the square side of the
boards, drawing a line from one to the other. Then
laying the boards open, the leaves must be tied near
to the back by winding a piece of fine cord several
times round from the head to the tail, to prevent the
leaves returning after the back is made flat to form
the gutter on the fore-edge. This done, beat the
back flat on the press, and place one of the cutting
boards at the end of the book, even with the line
before made; turn it, and place the runner as much
below the line on the title side, as has been allowed
for the square on the fore-edge. Taking the whole
in the left hand, the volume must be examined to
remedy any defects, should it not be regular and equal
on both sides, and then put into the press, the runner
as before even with the right cheek; taking care to
keep the other board projected above the left, equal
to the square allowed in front, so that, when cut
through, the fore-edge may be equally square with the
boards on each side. To make the larger volumes
flat on the back, it is usual, after tying round, to put
them by the fore-edge loosely in the press, the boards
resting on the cheeks, and beating the back slightly
with the hammer. After the fore-edge is cut, the
string is taken off, the back resumes its circular form,

and the edge in consequence presents a grooved appearance, which is called the *gutter.*

The above method is termed *cutting in boards;* but as it is not necessary to cut school books and common work in boards, on account of their thinness, it is usual to cut a number of them together on the fore-edge, round the backs, press them a short time, cut the heads and tails, colour or sprinkle the edges, and then back them. The boards are afterwards marked, holed, &c. as before directed, and, if not before squared with the plough, cut square with the large shears, the edge of the book being the guide. This is called *cutting out of boards.*

COLOURING OF EDGES.

Colouring the edge with one colour, equally sprinkling over, marbling, and gilding, come under this head ; and though the latter two are in large towns distinct trades, from their being intimately connected with the business of a binder, and necessarily performed by those in smaller places, it is important that they should be treated of in this place, being, as before observed, considered best to speak of each operation as required to be employed in binding. The style of ornament of this description must depend on the price allowed for the work, and will vary according to the taste of the workman and wish of the employer.

OF COLOURING AND SPRINKLING.

The colours most used are blue, yellow, and brown, and for old books, red, in preparing which, it is necessary to grind them in water very fine on a slab with a muller. Each colour is then placed in a separate vase, and mixed up with a little paste and water to the proper consistency for use. To procure a better edge, two drops of oil, and about an equal quantity of vinegar and water may be mixed with the paste.

In colouring the edges equally over, the boards at the head of the volume must be beat even with the edges, and the book rested on the edge of the press or table, then holding the book firm with the left hand, the colours must be applied with a small sponge, passing it evenly upon the edge, proceeding towards the back one way and the gutter the other, to avoid a mass of colour being lodged in the angle of the fore-edge. This done, the other parts are similarly coloured, the fore-edge being laid open from the boards, and a runner held firm above to prevent the colour searching into the book. It will be perceived that a dozen volumes may be done at the same time with scarcely more than the additional trouble of placing one above the other. For further security, and to prevent the colour searching into the books, it may be advisable to put them into the laying-press, and screw them moderately tight.

In sprinkling, it is usual to tie together a number of volumes with a board on each side of the outside books, or place them in the laying-press, first with the fore-edge upwards. Then with a large brush, similar to a *painter's*, dipped in whatever colour may be wished, and well beat on the press-pin over the pot till the sprinkle becomes fine, the edges are covered; the pin and brush are held sufficiently above the book, and the edge sprinkled by beating lightly at first, and stronger as the brush becomes less charged with colour, being careful that the spots are as fine as possible, the sprinkle being thereby made more beautiful. Several colours are sometimes used with very pleasing effect; some of these combinations will be described, and many others will readily occur to the workman as his taste may suggest.

COLOURS.

Of vegetable colours, and ochres, directions for mixing which have been given above, it will only be necessary to particularize the most approved and generally used substances; the liquid ones will require a more lengthened description.

BLUE.—Indigo and Prussian Blue, with Whiting for lighter shades.

YELLOW.—Dutch Pink, King's Yellow, and Yellow Orpine.

BROWN.—Umber, burnt over the fire.

RED.—Vermillion; or Oxford Ochre, burnt in a pan.

PINK.—Rose Pink; to make it brighter, add Lake.

GREEN.—The first and second mixed to any shade.

The liquid, or spirit-colours, will be found best for use, as the edges will not rub, which all other colours are liable to do. Some of the receipts are well known; but it being necessary to give a faithful record of the art, the whole of the colours used, and modes of preparation, will be presented.

BLUE

Two ounces of the best indigo, finely powdered, mixed with a teaspoonful of spirit of salts, and two ounces of best oil of vitriol. Put the whole into a bottle, and let it remain in boiling water for six or eight hours, and mix with water as wanted to the shade required.

YELLOW.

French berries, saffron, or faustic chips. Boil with a small portion of alum, strain, and bottle for use.

GREEN.

The two colours above will make an excellent green, used in proportions as the shade required. Another green may be made by boiling four ounces of verdigris and two ounces of cream of tartar till a good colour is produced.

ORANGE.

Two ounces of Brazil dust, one ounce of French berries, bruised, and a little alum. Boil in water and strain.

RED.

Brazil dust, half a pound; alum, two ounces, well powdered; boiled in a pint of vinegar and a pint of water till brought down to a pint. Strain and bottle.

PURPLE.

Logwood chips, in a proportion of half a pound to two ounces of alum, and a small piece of copperas, boiled in three pints of soft water till reduced a third, will make a good purple.

Brazil dust, submitted to the action of strong potash water, will make a good purple for immediate use, but will not keep.

BROWN.

A quarter of a pound of logwood, and the same quantity of French berries, boiled together. If a darker is required, add a little copperas.

With these colours, the edges of books may be sprinkled to almost an infinite number of patterns. A few will be given; for though fancy sprinkles are seldom used where the binder can get the edges of extra books marbled, they will be of use to those who would find marbling a work of too great preparation and expense for a small number of books.

RICE MARBLE.

This pattern has been so called from the use of rice, but linseed or bread crumbs will answer the same purpose. The rice is laid on the edge of the book according to fancy, and the edge sprinkled with any colour, the rice thus forming blank spaces. The edge may be coloured previous all over, or sprinkled with a lighter shade.

WHITE SPOT.

Take white wax and melt it in a pot, then with a brush throw some upon the edge of the book; when it is set, colour the edge with a sponge. Take the book and give it two or three smart knocks on the end of the press, when the wax will fly off, and a beautiful white spot remain. This pattern may be much varied by using two or three colours, or sprinkling the edge before the wax is thrown on, and after it is, again with other colours,

Whiting mixed with water to a thick consistency, will nearly answer the same purpose, and is less expensive than wax.

FANCY MARBLE.

Take a small portion of rose-pink, green, or any other vegetable colour, and well bray it on the slab with the muller, till reduced to a fine powder. Prepare a dish, or other vessel, large enough to admit the fore-edge of the book, and filled with clear water; then with the *palette knife* mix a portion of the colour with spirits of wine, and convey with the knife some of the same to the middle of the vessel, and allow it to flow gradually on the surface of the water. The spirit of wine will cause it to spread in a diversity of pleasing forms, when the edge of the book must be dipped in the same manner as for marbling, and a very neat pattern will be produced at a trifling cost, as no more colour need be mixed than wanted at each time.

GOLD-SPRINKLE.

After the edges of the book are stained with any of the colours above described, a good effect may be given by sprinkling with a gold liquid, made in the following manner :—Take a book of gold and half an ounce of honey, and rub them together in a mortar until they are very fine ; then add half a pint of clear water and mix them well together ; after the water clears, pour it off and put in more, till the honey is all extracted and nothing left but the gold ; mix one grain of corrosive sublimate with a teaspoonful of spirits of wine, and when dissolved put the same, with a little thick gum-water, to the gold, and bottle it, always shaking it well before using. When dry, burnish the edge, and cover with paper till the work is finished.

MARBLING EDGES.

This is an operation requiring much care and attention in the preparation of every article used, for if any part be faulty, it is impossible to make a good marble. The tools and utensils that will be required are—a trough, perfectly water-tight ; a little round stick ; a comb ; an earthenware cup for each colour and the other preparations ; a small brush for each ; and a marble slab and muller to grind the colours. A little stove is also desirable for burning such colours

E

as may require it; but as this can be done in a pan
on the fire of the office, it is not essential.

The shell, Spanish, and Anglo-Dutch marbles will
alone occupy attention here, being those used for
book-edges; but the description of the Dutch marble
will be reserved for the part on Stationery Binding,
in which department it is now only used.

The Size.—Put into a pipkin, or other vessel, a
quantity of linseed, and pour over it boiling rain-water,
stirring the same round with a stick or piece of birch,
till the size is of sufficient consistency to bear the
colours on its surface. Should it be too thick, which
a trial will enable the workman to judge, add more
water, and if the contrary, more seed. The latter
should be obviated as much as possible, by not putting too much water at first to the seed, as the size
getting cool will have little effect on what may be
afterwards added.

The Wax.—Cut a little bees-wax of the purest
quality into small pieces, and place in a vase on a
slow fire till melted; then pour gradually to it spirits
of turpentine, stirring them together till they acquire
the consistency of honey.

The Colours.—For marbling, mineral colours,
strictly speaking, should never be used, as, being too
heavy, they will sink to the bottom of the size. The
vegetable colours and ochres, particularized at page
33, are the most proper, to which may be added two
others, *Ivory black* and *Flake white;* though the
latter will be seldom required, the size left uncovered

by the other colours generally forming sufficient white. These must be ground in *rain* water as fine as it is possible; the excellence of the marble depending much on the clearness of the colours. Two or three drops of the prepared wax above described, according to the quantity of colour to be ground, must be well worked in during this operation. The effects of the wax will be to stay the colour and produce a much finer edge when submitted to the action of the *Burnisher*.

THE SHELL MARBLE.

Put a little of each of the colours as above prepared into separate cups, and add thereto a small portion of *ox-gall* and water, mixing them well up with the brush appropriated to each colour. This will be all that is necessary for the vein colours, or those intended to be thrown first on the size. To the upper ones, which drive the former into veins, and which are to form the shell, add two or three drops of *boiled linseed oil*, and mix well with the brush, so that it is fully incorporated with the colour.

The size must be then poured cold into the marbling trough, very carefully, to prevent any of the seed accompanying it, and experiment made with the colours to see if they act properly. A small portion is taken in the brushes, and thrown on the size by gently tapping against the fore-finger of the left hand, in the order it is desired to use the colours. Should they not spread over the surface sufficiently, more gall must be added, and if the contrary, more unmixed

colour. The same must be done with the upper
colours, as respects the oil ; if on trial the shell should
not be sufficiently developed, and the opposite if the
oil causes white spots, or breaks. These trials must
be made by taking the colour off with blank paper.

The colours acting properly, the first must be
carefully thrown on, then the second, third, &c., till
the whole of the surface of the size is evenly and completely covered. To give an example, which will
answer for any other pattern, an edge to correspond
with the end papers (generally the case) of a green
pattern, having blue and yellow veins, is desired ;
one of the latter colours is thrown on, and then the
other, both prepared without oil ; and finally the
green, having oil to form the shell, in such manner
as to completely cover the surface till the blue and
yellow are driven by it into an endless variety of veins.
All being thus disposed, the marbling is commenced
by beating the boards at the head even with the edge,
and holding the leaves together, dipping them into the
size. Withdrawing it immediately, the size adhering to the edge with the colour must be shaken or
blown off as speedily as possible, to prevent it running into the book. The tail is next dipped in a similar
manner. Before marbling the fore-edge the boards
must be laid back, and the edge flattened on the press,
holding the leaves firmly together at each end, taking
the colour with the same precautions, and replacing
the boards immediately after dipping. It will be
necessary, previous to throwing on the colour for each

dipping, to clear the size of all the colour left on the surface from the previous one, by taking it well off with waste paper.

An infinite variety of marbles might be added, but as the proceedings are the same as above described, the workman will be perfectly able to execute any pattern that circumstances may demand, attention to the ground and body colours, and the order in which they are used in the pattern, being only required.

SPANISH MARBLE.

This marble has of late years been very fashionable, almost superseding the above altogether. To form this edge, the colours must be thrown on in a similar manner, and the dark and light shades peculiar to it, formed by marbling the volume gradually, instead of submitting the whole surface at one time, as directed for the shell marble. The top colour must have more gall than for the shell marble and less oil. The effect is produced by dipping the edge about an inch, then drawing the volume slightly forward, which forms a darker shade, dipping another inch, and so on to the end. The taste of the workman, or the colours of the end papers, will suggest the space proper to dip at one time.

ANGLO-DUTCH MARBLE.

The proceedings to be observed in this pattern, now also much in use, are the same as to the preparation of the colours, with the addition of a little spirits of wine Should the pattern present numerous

spiral forms, the colours must be directed with a
pointed stick into volutes, by turning them at such
distances as may be required. But if the pattern is
of a jagged form—that is, the colours running into
each other, they must be laid on the size with quills,
or bent pieces of brass latten, as in the Dutch marble,
and the pattern formed with a comb made for the
purpose. This is done by drawing the teeth of the
comb across in various ways, which causes the body
and vein colours to take a jagged form, according to
the distance of the teeth one from the other.

The result of many years' experience produces con-
fidence in asserting that the directions here given for
executing the department of marbling, on which subject so much error has been propagated, may be fully
relied upon for producing the effect desired. The
proceedings may appear plain and simple; they are
so, but without great care and observation the workman's labour may be entirely lost. *Bad* gall, *hard*
water, and other things that, till experience has taught
better, may appear trivial, will not fail to cause the
worst results, and the labour of a day in preparation
will thus be thrown away, perhaps, for the want of a
little attention to minor particulars.

As a step to the attainment of mastery in the art,
let the workman divest himself of the various *nostrums*
he has been put in possession of by *interested* parties,
and give himself up with assiduity to the directions
above laid down; he will soon find, though failure,

from some of the causes alluded to, may at first, and
will at times, take place, ultimate success attend his
endeavours.

GILDING EDGES.

This description of edge is the best preservative
against external injury and damp. The fore-edge of
the book is first gilt. It is screwed as tight as possible between boards placed even with the edge in
the laying press, and the first operation is commenced
by scraping the edge perfectly smooth with a steel
scraper, round on one side, and flat on the other, for
the better execution of such parts as present slight
inequalities of surface. After the edge is well scraped,
it must be *burnished* with the agate, then coloured
over with red bole or chalk, ground in soap, rubbed
immediately dry with fine clean paper shavings, and
again well burnished. This gives a deeper appearance to the gilding, and hides any slight defect that
a white edge at times presents.

The gold is next cut on the gold cushion to the size
required, and each piece taken off with a small slip of
paper folded with one smooth edge, or an instrument
called a tip, by rubbing it on the head and attaching
the gold by gently pressing upon it. The *size* (prepared with the white of an egg in three times the
quantity of water, well beaten together) must then be
applied evenly on the edge with a large camel's hair
pencil, and the gold immediately placed thereon.
Should any breaks appear in the gold, other portions
must be applied with a piece of cotton wool.

A size made of writing parchment, applied warm, with six or eight drops of vitriol in a cup full of the size, is used by some gilders, but the former being more simple, and equally effective, will be found preferable.

After the edge is dry, it must be burnished lightly and carefully to avoid rubbing off any of the gold; and to insure this the better, a piece of tissue paper should be placed on the edge during the first operation. After this burnish on the edge itself until it is perfectly uniform and clear. The head and tail of the volume must be gilt with the same precaution, the back towards the workman.

Should the work be of that nature that it is desirable to give it the character of the period in which the book was written, or an additional degree of beauty and elegance, this part of book ornament may be pursued further in the manner we shall now describe.

GILDING A LA ANTIQUE.

After the edge is finished as above directed, and before taking out of the press, ornaments, such as flowers, or designs in compartments, must be stamped upon it in the following manner. A coat of size is passed quickly over with great precaution and lightness, and only once in a place, to avoid detaching any of the gold. When dry, rub the edge with palm oil, and cover with gold of a different colour to the first; then with tools used in gilding leather, warmed in the fire, proceed to form the various designs by firmly impressing them on the edge. The gold that has not been touched by the tools is then rubbed off with a clean cotton, and there remains only the designs the tools have imprinted, which produce a fine effect. This mode is, however, now seldom used, though almost all the books in the original binding of the sixteenth century are so executed.

GILDING UPON MARBLED EDGES.

This edge, which Dr. Dibdin, in his Bibliographer' Decameron, calls "the very luxury, the *ne plus ultra* of the Bibliopegistic Art," is one requiring great care and expertness in the execution. After the edges have been tastefully marbled, and not overcharged with colour, the book must be put in the press, and well burnished as before directed. The size must then be laid lightly on, to prevent unsettling the colour of the marble, by which the edge would be destroyed, and the gold immediately applied, and finished off as in other edges. When dry the marble is perceived through the gold, and presents an appearance of great beauty.

GILDING ON LANDSCAPES, &C.

When the edge is well scraped and burnished, the leaves on the fore-edge must be evenly bent in an oblique manner, and in this position confined by boards tied tightly on each side, until a subject is painted thereon in water colours, according to the fancy of the operator. When perfectly dry, untie the boards and let the leaves take their proper position. Then place the volume in the press, lay on the size and gold, and when dry, burnish. The design will not be apparent when the volume is closed, from the gold covering it, but when the leaves are drawn out it will be perceived easily, the gilding disappearing and a very unique effect be produced. The time and labour required makes this operation expensive, and consequently very seldom performed. It is, however, considered necessary to describe the proceeding, as the taste or wishes of some may render it necessary that the workman should know how to operate.

After the volume is gilt, the edges must be enveloped in clean paper, by pasting lightly the extremities one upon the other, to preserve the edges from injury in the subsequent operations. This is taken off when the volume is completed.

BLACK EDGES.

Books of devotion are generally bound in black leather, and instead of being gilt on the edge, blacked to correspond with the covers. It will therefore be necessary in this place to describe the process.

Put the book in the press as for gilding, and sponge it with black ink; then take ivory black, lamp black, or antimony, mixed well with a little paste, and rub it on the edge with the finger or ball of the hand till it is perfectly black, and a good polish produced, when it must be cleared with a brush, burnished, and cased with paper.

HEADBANDS AND REGISTERS.

The *headbnnd* is an ornament in thread or silk, of different colours, placed at the head and tail of a book on the edge of the back, and serves to support that part of the cover projecting above in consequence of the squares of the boards, giving to the volume a more finished appearance. Thus it will be seen that the headband must equal the square allowed for the boards. For common work the headband is made of paper well rolled between two boards, and slightly pasted to hold the paper firm; but for extra work, and volumes requiring greater durability, it is made of thin board and parchment pasted together and cut into *strips* of the breadth required. These flat head-bands produce a much better effect than the round ones.

There are two kinds of headbands, viz. single and double. For ordinary work cloth pasted round the band or common thread is used, for *extra*, silk and sometimes gold and silver thread. If the volume is small it is placed, with the boards closed and drawn down even with the edge, between the knees, or, if larger, placed at the end of the laying-press, with the fore-edge projecting towards the body of the work-man.

SINGLE HEADBAND.

Take two lengths of thread or silk, of different colours, threading one in a long needle, and tying the ends of the two together. Supposing red and

white to have been taken, the white attached to the
needle, it is placed in the volume five or six leaves
from the left side, and forced out on the back immediately under the chain-stitch of the sewing, and
the thread drawn until it is stopped by the knot,
which will be hid in the sheet; the needle is then
passed a second time in or near the same place, and,
after placing the prepared band under the curl thus
made, the thread is drawn tight, so as to hold it firm.
Before placing the band it must be bent with the
fingers to the curve of the back of the book. The
red thread is now taken with the right hand, and
bringing it from the left to the right, crossed above
the white thread, passed under the band, and brought
round to the front again, and fastened by passing
over it, in the same way, the white thread, taking
care that the *bead* formed by these crossings touch
the edge of the volume. In repeating thus alternately
the operation, crossing the two threads, and passing
each time under the band, which is thereby covered,
it must be occasionally fastened to the book by
inserting the needle as before directed, once in as
many places as the thickness of the book may require,
and giving it a double tack on the right side on com-
pleting the band, fastening it on the back with a
knot. These fastenings give firmness to the headband and the exact curve of the back. The two projecting sides of the band must be cut off near the silk,
giving the band a slight inclination upwards, to
prevent the work slipping off before covering.

DOUBLE HEADBAND.

This headband is made of silk of various colours, and differs from the single, both in being composed of two bands, a large and small one, and in the manner of passing the silk. It is commenced in the same way as the single, but when the bands are fastened, the smaller above the larger, the red silk is taken with the right hand and passed above the white, under the bottom or larger band, brought out under the upper or small one, carried over it, brought out again over the large band, and the bead formed as above directed, near to the edge of the book. The white silk is then passed in the same way, and so on alternately till the whole is completed.

GOLD AND SILVER HEADBAND.

Both single and double made as above, the only difference being in the use of gold or silver thread. Great care must be here observed in tightening the thread at the bead.

RIBBON HEADBAND.

This style varies but little from the other, the same coloured thread being only passed several times round, instead of alternately with the other, and making the bead at each turn, taking care that the under thread is not observed, and then passing the other colour in a similar manner, as many or more times than the former. This will produce a band, from which it is named, having the appearance of narrow ribbons, of various colours. Three or more colours may be used in a pattern. F

REGISTERS.

For those volumes which require only narrow rib-
bon, registers are not placed till after the completion
of the binding; but for those of a larger size, being
much used, it will be necessary to attach them under
the headband and glue one of the ends on the back
of the book, bringing the others down between the
leaves, and turning the part intended to hang out at
the bottom into the book again, to preserve them
from being soiled till the work is finished. For
books handsomely bound, such as Altar Services, &c.,
gold fringe is sometimes affixed to the ends of the
registers, which adds to the general effect of the
ornamental part of the binding.

OPEN BACKS, BANDS, &c.

The practice of cutting off the corners of the boards
next the headbands is now nearly discontinued.
Should it, however, be desirable to do so, they must
be cut slopingly off from the outside to the board
placed under, to prevent injury to the back and edge.
Cutting a piece off straight through with the shears,
produces a bad effect when the end paper is pasted
down. In *lining the back* the volume is placed by
the fore-edge in the laying press, and the back glued
lightly. A piece of cartridge paper is applied thereon,
one edge level with the side, and evenly rubbed with
the folding-stick, creased on the other side and cut off.
The book is then taken out of the press, the projecting paper cut off with the shears at the head and tail,
the headband rubbed close to the back, and the back

again slightly glued. If wished stronger, another fold must be glued on before cutting off. When a loose back is required, to allow the book to open with greater freedom, it will be necessary to glue the paper on as above, leaving projecting over so much as will exactly cover the back. Then fold the part so left evenly by the edge, and in like manner bring over the other part, which must be cut off evenly on the opposite edge. The two parts being glued, must then be rubbed well together, and the headband set with the folder. If it is wished that the volume should have raised bands, the back must be marked at equal distances with the compasses, or by means of a pattern cut out in pasteboard, when glueing again the back the bands must be placed. These bands are generally cut out of a piece of firm thick leather or pasteboard. When the glue is dry, cut off the part of the bands projecting over the sides, as also, when open backs, a short space down each fold of the paper, to admit that portion of the cover necessary to be turned in at the head and tail.

COVERING.

The skins prepared for binding are dressed in a peculiar manner; they are soft and of equal thickness throughout. The cutting out of covers is an important operation, as by attention much economy may be effected. For this purpose patterns in pasteboard of all the sizes of books should be made, and such as

are required placed on the skin, turning them every
way so as to obtain the greatest number of pieces
possible, allowing about half an inch round for pair-
ing and turning in.   Should the books be of the
same size, a volume taken by the fore-edge and the
boards laying open on the leather will enable the
workman to judge to a nicety the most advantageous
way to cut.   The narrow pieces, &c., left on the
sides will do for the backs and corners of half-bound
work.   Sheep-skin and calf for common binding
should be steeped in clear water and well squeezed
out, then stretched and extended on the table, the
smooth side upwards.   For law books the leather
must be cut out dry, damped with a sponge, and the
covers laid one on the other to preserve their moist-
ness, taking care not to twist them, which would
present marks in the binding.   This plan is advisable
for all extra calf work, the colours taking better and
far more uniformly.   Morocco and roan must not be
wetted, as it would destroy the grain and stain the
leather.   Russia must be well soaked with warm
water, but care taken to avoid creasing.   It will also
require to be well rubbed out on the table with the
folder.

Each cover must be pared round the edges with a
long knife, called the paring-knife, on a fine marble
slab, by extending it, the smooth side below, and
taking off the flesh side by moving the knife forward
diagonally from about half an inch of the edge gradually down to it.   The cover must be held firm with
the left hand, and care taken not to cut through the

cover before reaching the edge; but practice will soon render this easy. To obviate the difficulty which morocco and roan present in paring, from not being wetted, it is usual to slightly moisten the edges on the rough side of the leather. This is also sometimes done to rough calf, that is, where the leather is dressed on the flesh side of the skin, and more particularly used in stationery binding.

Whatever may be the substance or material with which a book is covered, the manipulations are the same. It is well pasted over with the brush and placed on the volume in the same way, care being taken to preserve from stains those that are costly and delicate, particularly morocco and silk, which will be again alluded to. If the covers that have been wetted before paring have become dry, they must be again sponged with clear water. They should then be placed on a board, and the side of the skin which is to be applied to the volume, pasted well and evenly upon the surface, leaving no more than what is necessary to make it adhere. The cover being then laid on a table, or clean milled board, the volume is taken in the hands, the squares at head and tail equally adjusted, and placed upon the nearest side of it, in such a position that the back of the volume, which is from the workman, will be in the middle. The far part is then brought over to the other side, and care taken not to disarrange the squares. The cover, which now projects about an inch all round the volume, is drawn tightly on the back with the open hands, as

F 3

also on the sides of the boards, which are rubbed with
a smooth folder to efface any marks or wrinkles that
may appear. The cover cannot be drawn on too
tightly, as it is indispensable that it apply well to
every part of the book, and that the superfluous paste
be forced to the edges of the boards. The book must
now be opened, the paste taken off, and the leather
projecting over the fore-edge turned in, every wrinkle
effaced with the folder, and the edges of the boards
rubbed square. Turn the book and operate in a similar
manner on the other side.

The cover at the head and tail of the book must
next be turned in, by taking it by the fore-edge, and
placing it upright on the table with the boards extended, and with the hands, one on each side, slightly
forcing back the boards close to the head-band, and
folding the cover over and into the back with the
thumbs, drawing in tight so that no wrinkle or fold
is seen. If the back is an open one, the loose part of
the fold, previously made, must be covered over with
the leather similar to the boards. Having turned in
the cover the whole length of the boards, and rubbed
it with the folder as on the fore-edge, the volume
must be turned and operated on at the bottom in a
similar manner.

The volume is now opened, and the parts of the
cover brought together at the corners, pulled up almost
perpendicularly with the board, nipped together, and
nearly all above the point of the angle of the corner,
cut off with the shears. The portion on the side is
then turned down, and the other on the fore-edge

wrapped a little over it, the corner being set by the
aid of the thumb-nail and folder as neatly as possible
The folder should also be well rubbed in the joints to
make the covers adhere in those parts, where the back
is liable to hold the leather off. Any derangement
of the square of the boards, that may have taken place
in covering, must here also be rectified.

The setting of the headband is the next operation,
which is very important to the beauty of the binding,
by properly forming a sort of cap over the worked
headband, of the leather projecting across the back a
little above a right line from the square of one board
to the other. With a small smooth folder, one end a
little pointed, the double fold of the leather must be
rubbed together to make it adhere, and if the boards
have been cut at the corners, the hand applied thereon, and finally forcing the headband close to the
leather, staying it even on the back with the finger,
and forming a neat cap of the projecting part on the
top of it. The folder is then applied on the edges of
the boards to give them a square appearance, and
make the leather adhere. Should any defect in the
leather make it necessary to apply another piece on
the part, it must be neatly pared, and pasted on at
this stage of binding.

Should the leather project from the board at the
joints the volume must now be *nipped* in the laying
press, between two boards, similar to cutting boards,
being thicker on one edge than the other, and so
placed on the joints that the thick side solely holds
the volume when pressed. When taken out, and the

leather appears nearly dry, the back must be rubbed with the folder, the headband corrected if required, and the volume again placed to dry.

A few observations must not be omitted relative to morocco, velvet, silk, and coloured calf, which, from their nature, require the greatest neatness to avoid stains and alterations in the colours. Covers of the former description must not be drawn on too tight or rubbed with the folder, as the grain or pattern of the material would thereby be destroyed; and extra care must be taken with the coloured calf to prevent damage. They must be drawn on with the hands on each side at the same time; the table should be covered with a baize cloth, and the hands perfectly clean. Silk should be prepared previously, by pasting a piece of paper thereon and be left to dry, so that, when pasted for covering, the damp will little or nothing affect its appearance. Velvet will require great care, from its peculiar texture making it necessary that it be rubbed one way only in covering. From this cause, having ascertained the direction of the *nap*, one side of the book is glued and laid upon it, and drawn smoothly on towards the back, then the back and other side is in like manner drawn over, and afterwards the edges turned in. This proceeding causes the whole to lay perfectly smooth, which velvet would not do, if drawn in a contrary way to the grain or nap.

If the book has been sewn on bands, or artificial ones have been glued on as directed, the projection prevents the leather adhering close to the back, which

must be remedied whilst the paste remains wet.
Where the bands are large, it will be necessary for
them to be *tied up,* which is done by placing a board,
longer than the book, on each side, projecting slightly
over the fore-edge, and tying them tightly with a
cord from end to end. Then with a smaller cord the
leather is confined to the sides of the bands, by crossing the string :—for example, suppose the book had
three bands, one towards the head, one towards the
tail, and the other in the middle ; the book would be
taken in the left hand, the head upwards, the cord
by the help of a noose passed round close to the
inside of the band nearest the tail and drawn tight,
then carried round again and brought close to the
other side. The string tightened is thus crossed on
the side of the volume, and the band held between
it. The cord is in like manner carried on to the
second and third bands, fastened, and the whole set
square with the folder. It will be best understood
by the following engraving.

If the corners of the boards have been cut off near
the headband, a piece of sewing thread tied slightly
round between the back and boards will be of advantage in causing the head and tail to set properly.
When the book is perfectly dry the cords are taken off,
the bands again rubbed and squared, and the department of FORWARDING completed.

For morocco, and books in other substances, having but small bands, tying up is not resorted to, being generally rubbed close in with the folder, or a box stick for the purpose. For morocco, however, where the beauty of the grain is liable to be destroyed, a *pallet* with single, double, or treble lines is sometimes used, warm, on each side of the band.

A few words may be added relative to the grain of morocco. If the natural grain is not sufficiently developed, it must be raised by rolling the leather, doubled, on the table with the hand. The turkey grain is formed by steeping the cover in water, rubbing it from corner to corner, and then contrary way, till the grain is brought up full and square.

HALF-BINDING.

Half-binding, so called from the back and corners only being covered with leather, and the sides with paper or parchment, presents no difference in the covering to what has been pointed out above. The leather to form the back should come down about one inch and a half on each side, and the corners neatly pared round before placing on. The sides of paper must not be pasted on till the binding is nearly finished, either before the back is gilt or after, to avoid damage. This paper is pasted, at equal distances from the back, according to the taste of the workman, and the size of the volume. When dry, the end papers are pasted down, and the work finished in the same way as will be pointed out for bindings in general.

ਹੁੰdy

PART II.

OF FINISHING.

INTRODUCTORY REMARKS.

We have now arrived at a branch of the art, not only requiring all the careful attention before enforced, but a considerable share of taste and talent; taste to form a true estimate of what will accord well with the nature of the work and add to the beauty of the binding; and talent to execute the colours and designs in the best manner. This department may be distinguished under two general heads—Colouring and Gilding. The remarks here made will equally apply to both; but a few separate observations on colours and leather, as applied in binding in the various departments of literature, will be proper in this place, reserving those on gilding till that subject is treated of.

The kind of leather and description of colouring must ever be dependent on the nature of the work, the wish of the employer, and the price allowed for the binding. For a small number of books, a variety of patterns will perhaps be the principal object sought, and elegance alone studied; but where a numerous collection of the treasures of literature is placed in the hands of the binder, it becomes a subject of consider-

ation to produce the best possible effect, by presenting an appearance of different colours and leather,
yet still displaying a general harmony throughout.
No fixed rule can be laid down for the binder's guid-
ance ; but if he possess good taste, that cannot fail to
be the best instructor.   But it may not be irrelevant
here to introduce the opinion of Dr. Dibdin, whose
connexion with some of the first libraries in this
country, and whose intimate knowledge of all the
great book collectors of the same, must tend to stamp
him as a good authority on the subject :—

" The general appearance of one's library is by no
means a matter of mere foppery, or indifference ; it
is a sort of cardinal point to which the tasteful collector does well to attend.   You have a right to consider books, as to their *outsides,* with the eye of a
painter ; because this does not militate against the
proper use of the contents.

" Be sparing of red morocco or vellum, they have
each so distinct, or what painters call spotty, an
appearance, that they should be introduced but
circumspectly.   Morocco, I frankly own, is my
favourite surtout; and the varieties of them, *blue*
(dark and light), *orange, green,* and *olive colour,* are
especially deserving of your attention.

" Let *russia* claim your volumes of architecture or
other antiquities, of topography, of lexicography, and
of other works of reference.   Let your romances and
chronicles aspire to *morocco* or *velvet ;* though, upon
second thoughts, *russia* is well suited to history and

chronicles. And for your fifteeners, or volumes printed in the fifteenth century, whether Greek, Latin, Italian, or English, let me intreat you invariably to use *morocco :* for theology, *dark blue, black,* or *damson colour ;* for history, *red* or *dark-green ;* while, in large-paper quartos, do not fail to remember the *peau de veau* (calf) of the French, with gilt upon marble edges! My abhorrence of *hogskin* urges me to call upon you to swear eternal enmity to that engenderer of mildew and mischief. Indeed, at any rate, it is a clumsy coat of mail. For your Italian and French, especially in long suites, bespeak what is called *French calf binding ;* spotted, variegated, or marbled on the sides ; well covered with ornament on the back, and, when the work is worthy of it, with gilt on the edges. Let your English octavos of history, or belles lettres, breathe a quiet tone of chastely gilded white calf with marbled edges; while the works of our bettermost poets should be occasionally clothed in a morocco exterior."

The further opinion of the Doctor on the style of ornament, &c. in gilding, will be given in its proper place, and which, with that cited above, may be safely acted upon by the binder, blended with such additions as his own taste may dictate.

It is in this stage that the defects of forwarding will become more apparent, and which no tact or ingenuity of the finisher can effectually remedy; for, unless the bands are square, the joints free, and the whole book geometrically just, the defect, whatever it

may be, will appear throughout, and tend to destroy
the beauty of every subsequent operation, from the
constraint required to make the general appearance of
the work effective.

The substances used for the covers of books, are, as
before stated, of various kinds. Those covered with
morocco, roan, russia, velvet, vellum, silk, or coloured calf, which latter has been brought to great perfection by the leather-dressers, will not require any
further operation till prepared for gilding. But the
cover of a book in plain calf, or sheep, would not be
agreeable if left the natural tan colour; and the taste
and ingenuity of successive workmen have discovered
many beautiful designs and splendid colours, which
add much to the appearance of the book. Latterly,
however, many of them have been little used, and particularly so since the introduction of coloured calf.
Still, the binder should be conversant with the proceedings, as many of the uniform colours may be
required, and the various designs which early volumes
may display, cannot be executed till after the book is
covered. Some of these are little understood; and
even the common marble, now only used for the
plainest bindings, at one time was a profound secret,
and great caution was used to keep it so, books being
sent to the inventor to be marbled at a high price.
The receipts given for the superior marbles and
designs, will, it is presumed, present this branch of the
art on a higher footing, in a general point of view,
than is usually accorded to it; and it is confidently

asserted, that not one of them will prove a failure, if
attention to the directions be only given. Nothing
has been omitted in the description of the substances
best for use, the mode of preparing them, and the
proceedings to be adopted, that can tend to give to
the covers all the elegance and splendour of which they
are susceptible. By the aid of these, assisted by some
taste, the workman may vary the designs almost to
infinity; but it must be admitted that unless he is devoted to his art, no mere directions or casual advantages will enable him to succeed in the more complicated or delicate operations, while with an ardour for
it, all difficulties will be easily overcome.

COLOURING.

There are three sorts of ornaments upon the covers
of books, independent of gilding and blind tooling;
viz. marbles, sprinkles, and uniform tints : these will
be described under separate heads, but previous to
doing so it will be necessary to make known the methods of preparing the chemical substances and ingredients required to execute them in the best manner.

CHEMICAL PREPARATIONS.

Under this head is included *aqua regii*, or killed
spirits, *nitric acid*, *marbling water*, and *glaire* prepared for marbling.

AQUA REGII,

So called from its power to dissolve gold, is a mixture of nitrous acid (aquafortis), and muriatic acid

(spirits of salts), deprived of its burning qualities by
block tin, which it dissolves. It is called by the
chemist *acid nitromuriatic :* the muriatic also contains
a portion of alkali, which gives to red a vinous tint,
and for which colour it is principally used.

The two substances should be of the purest quality,
of a concentration of thirty-three degrees for the nitric
acid, and of twenty degrees for the muriatic. They
must be mixed with the greatest precaution. Having
provided a clear glass bottle, the neck rather long,
capable of holding twice the quantity to be prepared,
place it upon a bed of sand, the opening at top, and
pour in *one part* of pure nitric acid and *three* of muriatic. Let the first vapours dispel, and then cover
the orifice with a small phial, which must not confine
the vapour too closely, as the bottle would be liable
to burst, but which retains as much as possible without risk. Of block tin, an eighth part of the weight
of the acid must then be dropped into the bottle, in
small pieces, a little at a time, covering the orifice
with the phial. The acid will immediately attack the
tin and dissolve it, when a second portion must be
put in with the same precaution, and so on till the
whole is dissolved. *Malacca* tin is the best for use,
and if pure there will be no sediment, but as it cannot always be obtained, a black sediment will be left.
The vapour having ceased, the acid must be poured
into bottles and secured with glass stoppers, to preserve it. When used, a part is taken and mixed with
one quarter of i s weight of distilled water.

It is usual with some workmen to perform this operation in a common drinking glass, but as the vapour is thereby all dispersed, the composition loses a considerable portion of its best quality, for it will be observed, if performed in a bottle as above directed, that the vapour assumes a red tint, which does not escape if the neck of the bottle be of sufficient length.

ANOTHER.

Some binders adopt the following method, but as it is not capable of producing an equal beauty and clearness of colour with the one above given, it will not be advisable to use. The former, too, will be equally effective to an indefinite period, while this will not preserve more than two or three months.

Put in a brown freestone pot two ounces of powdered *salammoniac*, six ounces of fine *Malacca tin*, in strips or drops, twelve ounces of distilled water, and last a pound of *nitric acid*, of thirty-three degrees. Leave the whole till the tin is dissolved, and then pour off and bottle as above directed.

VITRIOL WATER.

Vitriol, as sold in the pure state, will not be proper to use in marbling or sprinkling, as it would corrode and destroy the leather. It must be weakened at least in a proportion of one ounce of vitriol to three of water.

MARBLING WATER.

It is usual with many to use the water pure, but a few drops of *potash liquid* mixed with it will be found to produce better effect, the marble being rendered more distinct.

GLAIRE.

Put spirits of wine in a proportion of two drops to the whites of twelve eggs, and beat the whole well together till perfectly clear.

PREPARATION OF THE COLOURS.

The preparations used by different binders vary much, as will be seen by the receipts given for the same colours, which we judge necessary to put on record, that nothing connected with the subject should be omitted, premising that each colour may be depended upon for producing the most satisfactory results. It may be proper also to observe that the whole of the woods and other ingredients used should be previously powdered, or reduced to small pieces, the colours being thereby much better extracted.

BLACK.

1.—Dissolve half a pound of green copperas in two quarts of water. The oxide contained in the sulphate of iron will combine with the tanning of the leather, and produce a good black.

2.—Boil in a cast-iron pot a quart of vinegar, with a quantity of rusty nails, or steel filings, till reduced one-third, taking off the scum as it rises to the top. This liquid improves by age. To keep up the quantity, boil with more vinegar.

3.—A cheaper liquid may be produced by boiling two pints of beer and two pints of water, with two pounds of old iron, and a pint of vinegar, scumming as before, and bottling for use.

BROWN.

1.—Half a pound of good Dantzic or American potash dissolved in one quart of rain water, and preserved in a bottle well corked.

2.—Salts, or oil of tartar, in the same proportions as above.

3.—A beautiful brown may be procured from the green shells of walnuts. To prepare this, a quantity of the green shells, when the nuts are gathered, must be pounded in a mortar to extract the juice, and then put into a vessel capable of holding a sufficient quantity of water. The water being put in, the whole should be frequently stirred, and left to soak, with the vessel covered. Afterwards the liquid must be passed through a sieve, the juice well expressed, and bottled, with some common salt, for use. This liquid, after fermentation, will produce the best effects for the uniform tints, as it tends to soften the leather, and will not corrode.

BLUE.

1.—It is usual with many binders to use *Scott's Liquid Blue,* but it is necessary to know the preparation of the colour. Perhaps the best and most simple known is one given by *Poerner,* which is as follows:—In four ounces of sulphuric acid, of 66 de-

grees, mix gradually one ounce of finely powdered
indigo, so as to form a sort of pulp. Place the vessel in another containing boiling water, for some
hours, and then leave it to cool. Afterwards put to
it a small portion of good potash, dry and finely powdered, stirring the whole well, and letting it rest for
twenty-four hours, when bottle, and use as required.
This colour will appear nearly black, but may be
made to any shade by adding water to it. If any
portion remain after being diluted, it must be put
into a separate bottle, as if mixed with the first preparation the whole would be deteriorated.

2.—A readier blue may be prepared by mixing
one ounce of powdered indigo with two ounces of oil
of vitriol, and letting it stand for twenty-four hours,
and then adding twelve ounces of pure water.

PURPLE.

Boil half a pound of archill or logwood with vinegar and water, of each half a pint.

LILAC.

Same as for the purple, with the addition of about
two table spoonsful of potash.

VIOLET.

Half a pound of logwood chips, and one ounce of
brazil dust, boiled over a good fire in four pints of
water till reduced one-half, and left to clear. Then
throw in one ounce of powdered alum, and two grains
of cream of tartar, and again boil till dissolved. This
liquid must be used warm.

FAWN.

In two pints of water boil one ounce of tan and a like portion of nutgall till reduced to a pint.

YELLOW.

1.—To one ounce of good caked saffron, turmeric, or French berries, add a portion of spirits of wine or aqua regii, and leave the mixture to macerate. This liquid is used cold, and may be varied to any shade by adding water when required.

2.—In two pints of water put eight ounces of French berries, and boil till reduced one-half. Then pass it through a sieve or fine cotton, and add a small quantity of powdered alum and again boil, using it warm.

ORANGE.

In a pint and a half of potash liquid, boil a quarter of a pound of fustic chips till reduced one-half; then put in an ounce of good *annatto*, well beaten, and after boiling, a small portion of alum, and use warm.

GREEN.

1.—Liquid blue and yellow mixed, will best suit for general purposes.

2.—Dissolve in a bottle one ounce of verdigris in an ounce of white wine vinegar, and place the whole before a fire for four or five days, frequently shaking the bottle.

RED.

There are three sorts of red; viz. common, fine, and scarlet.

Common. 1 —In a tinned kettle boil half a pound of Brazil wood, eight grains of nutgalls, both powdered, and three pints of water, till the whole is reduced one-third. Then add powdered alum and sal ammoniac, of each one ounce, and when dissolved strain through a sieve. This liquid must always be used warm.

2.—Boil a quarter of a pound of Brazil dust, two ounces of powdered cochineal, and a little alum, in two pints of the best vinegar, till a bright red is produced. Use warm.

Fine. 1.—In three pints of water boil half a pound of Brazil dust, and half an ounce of powdered nutgalls. Pass the whole through a fine cotton, and replace the liquid on the fire, adding one ounce of powdered alum, and half an ounce of sal ammoniac. Give the whole another boil, and then add a portion of *aqua regii,* according to the shade desired, and use warm.

2.—A quicker and cheaper proceeding is by putting in a cup a portion of Brazil wood, and adding to it the *aqua regii,* letting it stand for a quarter of an hour to extract the colour.

Scarlet.—To one ounce of white nutgalls and one ounce of cochineal, both finely powdered, add two pints of boiling water. After boiling some time, add half an ounce of *aqua regii,* and use warm.

MARBLING.

Before proceeding to a description of the marbles, and other designs on the covers, coming under the general head of marbling, it will be proper to give a few directions, relative to some important matters required in the way of preparation. As the success of many of the designs depends upon the quickness with which they are executed, it will be important that the colours, sponges, brushes, &c., are previously disposed in the best order, so as to be of the readiest access. Attention should be paid to the probable quantity that may be required of each colour, as many of them will not be available for use another time.

The books should all be previously washed with paste and water, to which has been added a little pearl-ash liquid, and left to dry. After this they must be glaired equally over, and when dry placed upon the marbling rods, the sides of the books extending over, and the leaves hanging between. The rods must be placed on an elevation at the top, so as to allow the water to run gradually towards the bottom of the books ; and if the backs are required to be left plain, another rod, or piece of board, grooved to the shape of the back, placed on them. To avoid the scum arising from the beating of the brushes over the colours, it is better to rub the ends of the bristles on the palm of the hand, on which a little oil has been spread. These preliminaries being

settled, the operation of marbling commences, for
which we shall now give directions.

COMMON MARBLE.

The book being placed on the rods, throw on the
water prepared for marbling in large drops, with a
coarse brush, or bunch of quills, till the drops unite.
Then with a brush charged with the black liquid, and
beaten on the press-pin as directed for sprinkling the
edges, a number of fine streaks are produced by
throwing the colour equally over the cover. Afterwards the brown liquid must be similarly thrown
over. When the veins are well struck into the
leather, the water must be sponged off, and the book
placed to dry.

If the volume has been previously coloured with
any of the preparations before described, and it is
wished to produce a marble thereon, the brown must
be thrown on first, and then the black, as without this
precaution the marble would not strike, because of
the acid which forms part of the colours. This
observation being applicable to all the other designs,
it will not be necessary to again repeat it.

ANOTHER.

Throw on the vinegar black, then the brown, and
lastly a fine sprinkle of vitriol water.

PURPLE MARBLE.

Colour the cover two or three times with hot
purple liquid, and when dry, glaire. Then throw on

water, and sprinkle with strong vitriol water, which
will form red veins.

STONE MARBLE.

After throwing on the water, sprinkle boldly with
the black liquid ; then with a sponge charged with
strong brown, drop the colour on the back in three or
four places, so that it may run down each side in a
broad stream, and afterwards operate with vitriol
water on the parts the brown has not touched.

GREEN AGATE.

Sprinkle black in nine times its quantity of water,
in large drops over the whole surface of the cover,
and when the drops unite apply on the back at regular distances the green liquid, so that it may flow on
the boards and unite with the black.

BLUE AGATE.

Proceed as above, only substituting blue in place
of the green, weakened with water according to the
shade required.

FAIR AGATE.

Commence by sprinkling black in small drops at a
good distance from each other; afterwards sprinkle
equally over large drops of weak potash.

AGATINE.

Proceed as for the green agate, and then sprinkle
scarlet all over the cover: finally, throw on blue in small
drops, weakened in four times the quantity of water.

H

LEVANT MARBLE.

After the water, throw on the back brown in broad
streaks as directed for the *stone*, and then in like
manner the aqua regii. This will be found to imitate
closely the Levant marble.

PORPHYRY VEIN.

Throw on large drops of black diluted in double
the quantity of water. When the colour has struck
well into the leather, sprinkle in the same manner
brown mixed equally with water. Then apply a
sprinkle of scarlet, and afterwards large spots of
yellow, the liquid nearly boiling. Whilst these colours are uniting, throw on weak blue, and then aqua
regii, which, flowing together down the sides of the
book, will form the vein distinctly.

RED PORPHYRY.

Sprinkle with black in eight times the quantity of
water, very equal and in small spots Let it dry,
rub, and glaire. Then give two or three sprinkles of
fine red, and one of scarlet, and again leave to dry.
Finally, sprinkle scarlet in small spots, as equally as
possible.

GREEN PORPHYRY.

For this design the cover must be finely sprinkled
over three separate times, leaving the colour to search
and dry between each. The green must be brought
to the shade required by mixing with water. To
form a more elegant vein, sprinkle first with weak

black, and afterwards with green, and when dry with
fine red.

PORPHYRY.

This marble, imitating the *eye of the partridge*, is
executed by throwing on black in eight times its
volume of water, in small drops, but so close as to
just run into each other. When the black begins to
flow, sprinkle over brown mixed equally with water.
Let it dry, wash the whole with a sponge, and before
quite dry again give it two or three coats of fine red.
After being dry and well rubbed, sprinkle equally over
the surface large drops of aqua regii.

ANOTHER.

Colour the cover with red, yellow, blue, or green,
and, when dry, with black diluted as above; let this
also dry, and then sprinkle over large or small drops
of aqua regii. The eye of the partridge is properly
formed with blue sprinkled upon the weakened black,
and, when dry, with the killed spirit or aqua regii.

ROCK.

Throw on large drops of black prepared as for the
porphyry, and, when half dry, weakened potash in the
same manner. When dry again, sprinkle on equally
small spots of scarlet, and lastly aqua regii.

GRANITE.

Mix black in about fifty times its quantity of water,
and sprinkle equally over very fine, repeating it as it
dries five or six times. Then in like manner sprinkle

over with brown, and after rubbing well, glaire lightly
Finally sprinkle finely over with aqua regii.

TREE MARBLES.

These marbles, which were first executed in Germany, from whence they passed into England, are
formed by bending the boards in the middle, so that
the water and colours flow from the back and fore-
edge to the centre, in the form of branches of trees.
The name is also given to such as are made to imitate
the grain of the wood.

WALNUT.

Formed by sprinkling black and brown only, as for
the common marble.

CEDAR

After sprinkling as for the walnut, and before perfectly dry apply lightly a sponge presenting large
holes dipped in orange upon various places on the
cover, so as to form a description of clouds. Afterwards apply the fine red, with a similar sponge,
nearly upon the same places, and when dry give the
whole two or three coats of yellow, taking care that
each penetrates evenly into the leather.

MAHOGANY.

The proceedings are nearly the same as for the
walnut, the difference being merely in sprinkling the
black more boldly, and when perfectly dry giving two
or three uniform coats of red.

BOX.

In order to imitate the veins contained in box, the boards must be bent in five or six different places and in divers ways. After placing the book between the rods, throw on the water in small drops, and proceed as for the walnut. After being perfectly dry, throw water again in large drops, and sprinkle on small spots of blue, diluted equally with water; and when again dry and rubbed well, apply the scarlet with a sponge as directed for the cedar. Finally, when dry, give two or three coats of orange, and the design is complete.

WAINSCOT.

Colour with strong brown, glaire, and place between the rods, with the boards flat. Throw on weak black in large spots, then brown in like manner, and lastly sprinkle boldly with vitriol water.

VARIEGATED.

Marble as for the walnut, and then put on each board a circle, oval, or other figure, and apply weak black on the outer parts. When dry, give it a good coat of red, and after throwing on spots of scarlet, take off the figures, and wash well the parts where the latter colour has been used. Finally, give the oval two coats of yellow, or other colour, with a camel's-hair brush.

MARBLING ON PAPER.

The sides of a half-bound book, which will be covered with paper, may be marbled to correspond

with the effect produced on the leather by the action
of the black and brown, at the same time. This is
performed by pasting firm white paper on the sides,
and colouring with a mixture of four ounces of nutgalls, and a small portion of powdered salammoniac,
boiled well together, which will take the black and
brown nearly equal to leather.

SPRINKLES.

This is another ornament on the covers of books,
capable of being much varied. A few of the most
general use are given, premising, that any of the colours arranged as for the marbles above, or sprinkled
on the uniform colours, will be productive of a beautiful effect. The books must be paste-washed over,
but not glaired.

NUTMEG.

Sprinkle very finely with black and then with
brown. If wished to produce a finer effect, give a
sprinkle of vitriol water.

RING.

Put about a teaspoonful of vitriol to a cup of the
black, and sprinkle coarsely over. If the ring is not
sufficiently strong, add more vitriol.

TORTOISESHELL.

Wash the cover with yellow, and sprinkle very
boldly with black. When dry, spot with a sponge,
as before directed, with blue, red, and black, each
colour being left to dry before the next is applied.

In concluding the description of the marbles and sprinkles, it may be remarked, that, with a little taste, the workman might vary the designs to upwards of one hundred different patterns ; also that each colour should be allowed to properly strike into the leather before another is used. Panes, or blank spaces, are formed by placing squares, &c. of pasteboard on the sides, which prevents the colours touching the leather when sprinkling. After the design is completed, the covers should be well rubbed with a woollen cloth, or the ball of the hand, to remove the whole of the refuse of the colour, which will be found to corrode on the surface of the leather.

UNIFORM COLOURS.

Before proceeding to execute any of the colours, the books must be well and evenly paste-washed, and left till perfectly dry. It will also be necessary to observe, that the black will become darker in all the subsequent operations of colouring, glairing, and polishing, so that attention must be paid not to use this liquid too strong.

LIGHT BROWN.

Wash the cover with vitriol-water, till perfectly uniform in colour, and then with brown to the shade desired.

ANOTHER.

Mix a small quantity of annatto with the potash liquid, and use hot. This will produce a beautiful tint.

DARK BROWN.

Colour with weak black till a slate shade is produced, and then apply the brown three or four times, as taste may dictate.

Others might be added, but the proceedings are the same, varying only the quantity of colour according to the shade. The *nut-brown liquid* will produce beautiful tints.

CORINTHIAN GRAPE.

The proceedings are the same as for the last colour, adding two or three coats of *fine* red.

COMMON GRAPE.

Proceed as for the last, omitting the brown after the black.

BLUE.

After giving four or five coats of the chemical blue diluted with water, wash lightly with weakened aqua regii, which will take off the green reflection produced by the yellow tint of the leather.

GREEN.

Give three or four coats of the green liquid, extended in water according to the shade required. Any of the other colours noticed in the preparations may be thus executed.

OLIVE.

After giving a slate colour, apply yellow, boiled with a small portion of blue, on the cover, rubbing it equally in while hot, to insure uniformity.

PEARL GREY.

This colour must be executed carefully, so as to be perfectly uniform and without stains. Colour over with exceedingly weak black liquid, till a pale grey is produced. The weaker it is, the better will the workman succeed. Then pass over a light coat of fine red mixed in a large portion of water, so as to give a light red reflection, scarcely distinguishable.

SLATE.

Use the black liquid, a little stronger than for the last, and omit the red.

BLACK.

For common purposes, the black may be formed in the way adopted for other colours; but, in many instances, it is necessary to produce a colour having the appearance of japan, and which will require more labour and attention.

Wash the book over with brown till a dark shade is formed; then, with a piece of woollen cloth, apply the black liquid mixed with japan, which will produce a beautiful black. This colour should have a good coat of vellum size before glairing. Or it may be better to finish off with the varnish given in another part of the work.

Nutgalls, copperas, and gum arabic, are used by many, and will be found to produce a good and bright colour.

GOLD MARBLES, LANDSCAPES, &c.

These designs, if properly executed, are the most beautiful that can be imagined. The labour and care, however, requisite, must ever confine them to superior bindings, for which a high price is given, to indemnify the workman for the time required to produce the proper effect. The imitation of the gold marbles is not an easy task ; but a knowledge of the art of painting, and a clever management of the brush, will enable the workman to imitate the figure of the marble so true to nature as to be scarcely distinguishable.

GOLD MARBLE.

This marble, which will not require the ability to execute as those following it, is the invention of *M. Berthé, senior,* bookbinder, of Paris, and may be executed on any kind of uniform substance. Take a piece of cloth, exceeding the size of the volume, and fold it equally ; lay it thus folded evenly upon a board, and then open the other half, and cover the board ; spread, upon the half towards the left, gold leaf, to the size of the cover, allowing such portion as the roll intended to be worked on it may take, which will be a saving of gold ; then refold the cloth on the gold, and press the hand above, without moving the cloth, so as to divide the gold into a number of small pieces. The gold being thus prepared, moisten the side of the volume with glaire, mixed with water in equal proportion, and place it on the cloth, pressing above firmly with the hand. Care being taken not to disarrange it, turn over the volume, cloth, and board, and take the latter off, replacing it with a sheet of paper, and rubbing smartly above, so as to attach the whole of the gold to the cover. After this the cloth must be removed, and the gold will be found equally fixed; to further insure which lay on a sheet of paper, and rub well with the palm of the hand.

To remove any gold that may appear on the part intended for the roll in gilding, wet the end of the thumb, form a sort of square with the fore-finger on the edge of the board to the size of the roll, and rub the surface of the cover, which will clear it with facility before the glaire is dry.

LAPIS-LAZULI.

This marble is of clear blue, veined with gold, presenting an appearance of the utmost splendour. It is executed as follows :—

Place the volume between rods as for marbling, and with a sponge, full of large holes, dipped in chemical blue, mixed in six times its volume of water, make light spots similar to clouds, at irregular distances; then put in a quarter part more blue, and make new clouds or spots a little darker. Repeat this operation six or seven times, each time adding more blue. All these coats will form stains in pro-

per gradation, as in the natural marble ; and to operate more properly, it would be better to have a
model, either of the marble itself, or skilfully
painted.

The veins of gold, which must not be laid on till
the book is gilt, and just previous to polishing, are
formed with gold in shell.   The substance used to
make it take and hold firmly on the cover of the
book, is prepared with white of egg and spirit of
wine, in equal proportion, and two parts of water,
beating all well and leaving it to clear ; then wet a
small portion of gold powder with the liquid, mixing
it with the finger, and use it with a small camel's-
hair pencil.   Pass it on in different places, so as to
imitate the model, according to the taste of the workman ; when done, let it perfectly dry, and polish with
the polisher scarcely warm.

It will be perceived, that by the use of other
colours, or two or three together, many beautiful
designs may be in like manner executed.

LANDSCAPES.

Many beautiful subjects may be formed on the
sides of books, by the workman skilled in painting.
The volume is prepared by being pastewashed, so as
to present an uniform fawn colour, the designs
slightly traced, and afterwards coloured according to
the pattern, the colours being mixed to the proper
shade with water.   The shades must be tried on

pieces of refuse leather, as, being spirit-colours, when once laid on, no art can soften them down if too strong, and a peculiar lightness of touch will be necessary to produce effect. Portraits, &c. may also be executed in this manner, and many superb designs have at times been executed by the best binders of this country and France. M. Didot, bookseller of Paris, presented a copy of the " *Henriade*," published by himself, to Louis XVIII., most elegantly ornamented in this style. It was executed by *M. Lunier Bellier*, bookbinder of Tours, and presented on one side a miniature portrait of Henry IV., and on the other a similar one of Louis XVIII., both perfect likenesses. The greatest difficulty consisted in the portraits, which were first imprinted on paper, very moist, and immediately applied to the cover, on which they were impressed with a flat roller. When perfectly dry, they were coloured with all the art of which the binder was capable, and the other ornamental paintings executed by hand. This proceeding requires great care in the execution, and will be applicable to any design where the binding will justify the expense.

TRANSFERRED LANDSCAPES.

The art of transferring, long practised in the ornamenting of fancy articles, was judged equally practicable for forming a superior embellishment for the sides of books. But the varnish necessary to be employed in the operation, rendered the invention of no utility, from the action of the heated polisher turning it white or causing it to shell off. After several trials, this difficulty is believed to be overcome, by the employment of a very simple and common article in the office of the bookbinder, viz. *new glaire*, well beaten up. The proceeding is as follows :—Cut the print, intended to be transferred, close to the design on all sides. Let it steep in the glaire till it is well saturated with it. During this time glaire the book twice, letting it dry on each application. Take out the print, place it exactly in the centre of the side cover, and, laying a piece of paper above, rub it sharply on the book so that it may adhere very closely. Remove the upper paper, and with the finger rub off the paper gently until the printed design begins to appear, wetting the finger in *glaire* should the paper get too dry. The utmost attention will now be necessary, for the least carelessness in removing the paper that still remains may entirely destroy the design, and the whole of the previous labour be lost. The paper must be gently removed, piece by piece, till the design only appears on the leather while damp. When dry, a white appearance will be presented, arising from the small particles of paper adhering to the ink, but these will be sufficiently hid on glairing the side previous to finishing. The extent and variety to which, at a small expense, these designs may be carried, with the finish and beauty given to the sides of books, renders the subject worthy of the attention of the ornamental workman particularly; but he must possess perseverance and carefulness in an eminent degree, to carry it to perfection. After the gilding or other ornament is executed, the side must be finished off in the usual manner. A slight coat of the varnish described in a subsequent part of the work, will, in this case, give a superior finish.

ETRUSCAN.

This style is, where, instead of covering with gold, the book is ornamented with gothic or arabesque compartments, or imitations of Greek borders and Etruscan vases, in their proper colours; which, when well executed, have a good effect. The Marquis of Bath possesses a copy of " *Caxton's Recuyell of the Historyes of Troye,*" bound in this coloured manner by *Whittaker*, of London, who some years ago brought the style to considerable perfection. The back represents a tower, in imitation of stone, on the battlements of which is a flag bearing the title, and on a projection of the tower the name of the printer is impressed. On the sides are Trojan and Grecian armour, in relief, round which is a raised impression of the reeded axe. The insides, which are also of russia, are ornamented with drawings, in India-ink, of Andromache imploring Hector not to go out to fight, and the death of Hector. The edges of the leaves are gilt, on which various Grecian devices are painted.

To execute this style properly, the design must be well marked out, and the colours prepared to the

proper shade by trials on refuse pieces of the same
material as that on which it is wished to operate.

ORNAMENTAL BLACK LINES.

Black lines, in rays, or intersecting each other in
the form of diamonds or other devices, on the sides
of books, which present a good appearance if well-
executed, are ruled with steel or swan pens, the nibs
being formed to the size required by the boldness of
the lines.　The vinegar-black, mixed with a portion
of gum-arabic, to neutralize a part of the action of
the acid and make it of stronger consistency, will be
found to answer best.　Whatever the pattern, it
should be slightly traced with the folder, and the
design be afterwards marked with the pen, kept
steady by the aid of a ruler.

BLACKING THE SQUARES.

Unless coloured uniformly, the whole of the designs
before described will not produce the best effect if
the squares remain plain or variously tinted; it is
therefore necessary to black the edges and squares of
the board, and the cap over the headband.　This is
done with a piece of any firm soft substance on the
edges, and with a sponge within the volume, sufficiently below the part where the end papers will
cover.　Finally, the covers should be well paste-
washed and left to dry.

BANDS AND TITLE-PIECES.

Where the backs are plain, it will be necessary to mark the places intended for the bands in gilding. For this purpose the binder should have patterns of the various forms and sizes cut out of thin board, a little longer and double the breadth of the volumes, so that they may be held firmly on the sides, while the bands are marked across the back through the apertures cut in the pattern. It is usual to give a double band at the bottom of the back, and therefore this must be allowed for in the pattern, which lengthened portion must be placed even with the edge of the boards at the tail of the volume, and the bands marked with the folder. By this plan the whole of the bands in sets of books will present a parallel line, and the bad effect produced by the inequalities arising from compassing the distances and trusting to the sight will be avoided. A great saving of time is also effected, as the patterns once made will serve for a very considerable period.

On the fancy colours and sprinkles it is usual to attach lettering-pieces of morocco. For this purpose the morocco, or roan if common work, is cut lengthways of the grain, according to the space between the bands, and the slip placed across the back to measure the breadth, and then cut off. Then slightly damping on the flesh side, it must be pared as thin and equal as possible, and the edges sloped evenly down so as to bring it to the exact size of the square it is to occupy. Should the back require two pieces, viz. another for the volume or contents, it may be proper to vary the colour. These title-pieces are pasted evenly on, a portion of paste rubbed over them with the finger, and then attached firmly and equally by rubbing down the edges with the folder, when the whole must be well washed off with a clean sponge. Where economy is an object, the squares intended for the title may be darkened with brown or black, which will show the lettering very well.

INLAID ORNAMENTS.

To give some bindings in vellum, calf, or morocco an additional degree of splendour, it is sometimes required to execute ornaments on the covers of a different colour, and as this is an important manipulation it will be necessary to give an example. Suppose we wish to make a rosette of eight sections on the side, the exterior circle of which is purple, and the leaves red, on which a gilding tool of the following pattern, but of larger dimensions, is to be impressed in gold.

Imprint the tool upon purple morocco, taking care that it marks the figure well, then cut it round on the exterior edge, and pare it evenly and very thin. Cut out and pare the leaves and the interior circle of the rosette, in red morocco, in the same manner. Then paste on the purple in the centre of the board, and when dry again impress the tool, to mark the places for the other nine pieces, which paste on evenly. The book will then be ready for gilding, and when covered with the gold ornament, the joints of the leather will not be perceptible, if well executed. Each leaf and the circle may be formed of different colours. The proceeding will be the same for forming bands on the back, or corners on the side, of other colours, paying attention to the forms and figures of the gilding-tools. This kind of ornament is more frequently executed on white vellum than any other substance.

BURNISHING.

Previous to gilding the covers, it is usual to burnish the edges, and paste down the end papers, though sometimes these operations are not performed till after. The edges are burnished by placing the volume open, with the fore-edge between boards, similar to backing boards in the laying press, and screwing it tightly therein; then with the burnisher rubbing the edge firmly and smartly over till it presents an uniformly bright surface, and free from any dents or inequalities. When the fore-edge is finished, the volume must be taken out of the press, and the head and tail burnished in a similar manner, the ends of the boards resting in the groove by the joints, the covered boards of the volume being open. Common

calf, sheep, and half-binding, may be burnished with
the boards closed, six or eight together, but it will be
necessary to delay pasting the sides on the latter till
after the operation, to avoid the liability of tearing.

PASTING THE END PAPERS, JOINTS, &c.

The volume being laid upon the table or press,
with the head towards the workman and the upper
board open, the guard or false end paper must be
removed and all other substances cleared out of the
joint with the folder. The end paper must then
be pasted over, and the cover brought down upon it,
pressed firmly, and again opened. It will attach
itself to the board, when it must be pulled down sufficiently to form the square and fold in the joint.
The position being adjusted, a piece of white paper
should be laid thereon, and the whole rubbed perfectly even with the flat of the hand. Then with the
folder the paper is slightly pressed into the crease
formed by the board and back, and rubbed perfectly
square on the joint. The volume with the board open
may then be turned, and the other side done in the
same way.

If it is intended to execute a gilt border or blind
tooling in the interior of the cover, it will be important that no part of the end paper covers it. To
avoid this a slip must be cut off at the head, tail, and
on the fore-edge, proportionate to the extra breadth
of the border over the square. Or, if morocco joints
have been placed in the volume, the two corners of

the portion left to be attached to the boards must be cut, to prevent their showing above the end paper, which is to be pasted over and would disfigure the edge, taking care to leave as much leather as will cover perfectly such portion as is intended for the joint and square of the board, so that, when the paper is pasted on, it will not be perceived that the corners have been cut off. Pare the edge of the leather where the part is cut off, on a small board or folder placed underneath; afterwards paste the joint on the edge of the board, attach it neatly with the thumb, finger, and folder, and when dry paste thereon the marbled or coloured paper, cut to the proper size.

For ordinary volumes common flour paste will do, but for silk, satin paper, and other delicate substances, it may be necessary to use a finer article which dries more quickly. In this case, use the finest gum arabic, dissolved in warm water; but very white starch, mixed strong, and without lumps, will be found preferable, as it soon dries and is not so liable to stain as the gum.

If the ends are of silk, it will be necessary to paste thereon a piece of white paper previous to placing on the volume, to avoid the stains which the acid entering into the composition of the leather is liable to make on the silk. This is also necessary in order to its being cut without presenting a jagged edge. When compassed and cut to the size of the square left within the ornamental border, usual in such bindings, it is

pasted on the paper side and placed evenly on the
board, rubbed firmly down, and left to dry. In all
cases, however, where the border is gilt or otherways
ornamented, below the level of the edges of the volume, the ends must not be pasted down till after that
operation is completed, as the glaire and oil would
be liable to stain, and present a bad effect. Where
the end papers are left plain, the last two leaves being
merely pasted together, the ends will only require
pasting, and attaching by placing the volume between
boards, and screwing firmly in the standing press,
immediately after which it must be taken out and the
boards opened, so as to make the joints free.

GILDING.

Before proceeding to a description of the various
manipulations required in gilding a book, it will be
necessary to direct the attention of the young workman again to what has been advanced relative to care
and attention in previous parts of this work, and follow up the remarks there made, with others on the
taste necessary to be displayed in this most important
part of the Art of Bookbinding. When it is considered that the most celebrated artists have arrived
at the eminence awarded to them, not only through
the elasticity, solidity, and squareness of their bindings, but also from the judicious choice of their ornaments for gilding, and the precision and beauty with
which they have been executed, it cannot be too

strongly impressed on the mind of the workman that this should ever occupy his first attention. Nothing is so disagreeable to the eye as injudicious or badly executed ornaments, while with chaste and classical embellishments, tastefully applied, an appearance of richness is produced on the volumes that cannot fail to give satisfaction to the most fastidious critic. The sides of the volumes present the field most favourable for the display of ornamental taste, admitting, from their extent, the execution of the most complicated designs. This elaborate style of ornament has been carried to such perfection and splendour as, in many instances, to have occupied several days in the execution of one side alone, but it is only by the most vigorous application, greatest care, and correct taste, that proficiency therein can be attained ; with these, success will soon crown the endeavours of the workman, and he will have the satisfaction of finding himself able to imitate any pattern, however difficult, as well as execute many new designs and compartments, of which, till he applied himself, he had not previously an idea.

As regards the style of ornament, it must be left to taste, but, as before promised, it will now be proper to introduce the remarks of Dr. Dibdin on the general effect of Gilding and Blind Tooling, leaving the detail to be suggested to the mind of the Gilder.

" First, let your books be well and evenly lettered, and let a tolerable portion of ornament be seen upon the backs of them. I love what is called an *over-charged back*. At first the appearance may be flaunt-

ing and garish; but time, which mellows down book
ornaments as well as human countenances, will quickly
obviate this inconvenience ; and about a twelvemonth,
or six months added to the said twelvemonth, will
work miracles upon the appearance of your book.
Do not be meagre of your ornaments on the back,
and never suffer *blind tooling* wholly to pervade a
folio or quarto, for by so doing you convert what
should look like a *book* into a piece of mahogany fur-
niture.

" In large libraries there should not be too much
blind tooling, or too great a want of gilt.   No doubt
the ornament should be as appropriate as possible to
the book.   One could not endure gingerbread gilt
Bibles and *Prayer Books,* or *Chronicles* or *Diction-
aries,* or other books of reference.   Let these have a
subdued decoration on their backs ; bands only full
gilt, or a running edge tool in the centres of them,
with small ornaments between the bands.

" I would recommend the lettering of a volume to
be as *full* as possible, yet sententiousness must sometimes be adopted.   The lines should be straight, and
the letters of one and the same form or character
within the line ; yet the name of the author may be
executed a size larger than that of the date or place
of its execution, and the lettering may be between
the top and bottom bands, or it may occupy the
spaces between three bands, or even more.   Re-letter
old books perpendicularly, as was the custom.   In
all fresh bindings, however prefer horizontal to perpendicular lettering.'

It remains to urge only that particular attention be paid to the letterings of books being their right titles, as the contrary will present to the judicious an effect the most disagreeable, and may be the cause of producing dissatisfaction with the whole of the binding in the mind of the owner ; and also to avoid the contrast which the different shade or colour of new lettering pieces will give to some bindings.

PREPARATIONS FOR GILDING.

To operate successfully it will be necessary that the workman provide himself with good size, glaire, and oil. The first is prepared by boiling fine vellum slips till a good size is produced, of a consistency that will lay equally on the volume without blotches or ropes, and must be used hot. The glaire is formed of the whites of eggs, beat well with a *frother* till it is perfectly clear, and the froth taken off. Some binders put a little spirits of wine in the glaire, in the proportion of one drop to six eggs. This liquid will improve by keeping, and should never be used new if it can possibly be avoided. For morocco bindings the glaire is sometimes diluted with water. The oil adopted by various binders is different, but palm oil, in its imported state, will be found the best for calf--sweet oil for morocco and Russia. Hog's lard is also considered good. For very light coloured calf fine mould candle is preferable.

Vellum size is now very seldom used in gilding. The best preparation for coloured calf is paste mixed

K

with urine. On books thus prepared the glaire must be applied twice, taking care that each coat is quite dry before the next is added, and that it lays perfectly even on the whole surface, free from globules or any substance whatever. Morocco and roan will not require more than one coat, and where practicable only on such parts as are to be gilt. The state of the weather must ever determine the number of volumes to be proceeded with at one time, as in the winter double the number may be glaired to what the dryness of a summer's day will admit of, so as to work with safety and produce effect. A good paste-wash before glairing is always advisable, as it prevents the glaire from sinking into the leather. The volumes being thus prepared,

GILDING THE BACK

is commenced, by oiling slightly, with a small piece of cotton, the whole length and the caps of the head-bands. If the book is merely intended to be *filletted*, for the economy of the gold, small strips are cut on the gold cushion, attached to the heated fillet by rolling it slightly over, and affixed to the volume by passing it firmly on the lines previously marked. But if the back is to be fully ornamented, it will be necessary to cover it entirely with gold.

The tools, &c., necessary for the gilder will be described in another section. These should be disposed on the table before him, so as to be selected with the greatest facility, and in readiness for every purpose for which they may be required.

On laying on the gold, the workman takes a book
of the metal, opens the outside leaf, and passes the
knife underneath the gold ; with this he raises it,
carries it steadily on to the cushion, and spreads it
perfectly even by a light breath on the middle of the
leaf, taking care also that not the least current of air
has access to the room he may be operating in. Afterwards the gold must be cut with the gold knife to
the breadth and length of the places to be covered, by
laying the edge upon it, and moving the knife slightly
backwards and forwards. Then rub upon the back
the oil, and apply the gold upon the places to be ornamented with a cotton or tip, rubbed on the forehead or hair to give it a slight humidity, and cause
the gold to adhere. But if the whole of the back is
to be gilt, it will be more economical to entirely
cover it, by cutting the gold in slips the breadth of
the book, and applying the back on it ; afterwards
press it close with the cotton, with which any breaks
in the gold must also be covered, by placing small
slips where required. The humidity of the hair or
forehead will be sufficient to make the gold adhere to
the cotton or other instrument with which it may be
conveyed to the book. The fillet or roll must then
be heated to a degree proper for the substance on
which it is to be worked. Calf will require them
hotter than morocco and roan, and these warmer
than russia and vellum. To ascertain their proper
heat, they are applied on a damp sponge, or rubbed
with the finger wetted, and by the degree of boiling

K 2

that the water makes their fitness is known; but a
little exercise and habit will render this easy of judg-
ing. To further insure this, the roll or pallet is
passed over the cap of the headband : if too hot,
the gold will be dull; if too cool, the impression will
be bad, from the gold not adhering in every part.

When the headbands are gilt, and the gold is found
properly fixed, the volume is placed against a piece of
wood in the form of a **T**, screwed tightly in the laying press, the top about an inch below the level of
the back of the book when placed, with the fore-edge
resting on the press, against it. The pallet or roll
intended to form the bands, must then be worked
gradually across the back, describing the arc of a
circle, guided by the places previously marked for the
bands, and forming a double one at the tail, for which
the larger space was allowed. Care must be taken
that every one present a parallel line to the other, so
as to avoid the disagreeable effect produced from an
inclination to either side. It will also be necessary to
rub each tool on a piece of rough calf before using,
that the gold may present a bright appearance in
every part.

The book must now be placed evenly in the laying
press, and the ornamental tools worked off. In
placing these, great attention should be paid to their
occupying the exact centre of the squares between
the bands. If the ornament is not large enough to
fill the whole square so as to present an agreeable
effect, one of the smaller tools, corresponding in

detail, must be chosen to fill up the corners or other spaces left. This will be fully descanted on under the head of Combination of Tools. Should it be desired to present on the back simply an ornamental lettering-piece at the head, diverging to a point towards the middle of the book, and the rest of the volume left plain, it will be necessary to impress the tool previous to glairing, and then apply the glaire with a camel's hair pencil in the indentations the tool has formed. When dry, cover with gold, and re-impress the tool in the marks previously made, and letter the title. This proceeding is adopted in every pattern where part of the back is intended to be left dull, by being free from glaire.

The judicious choice of ornaments for the back is of the utmost importance. For instance, such as represent animals, insects, or flowers, which are only proper for works of natural history, entomology, and botany, should never appear on the backs of works on general literature, as it would be an evidence of bad taste or carelessness.

The title must next engage attention, and the letters placed thereon, either singly or together, with brass type properly fixed in the hand chase. If with single letters, the tail of the volume must be lowered about an inch, and the workman, unless very experienced, will do well to draw a thread of silk across the gold to direct the heads of the letters. Taking each singly, he places them on the back with the right hand, steadying the letter with the forefinger of the

K 3

left. If the title is set in the chase, and the volume
not thick, it may be lettered in a similar manner to
that described for the pallets or rolls, by placing it
against the board, and lettering it across gradually;
but if thick, it will be better to place the volume
evenly in the press, and apply the title, guided by the
thumb, firmly across. The title in either case must
be justified to produce the best effect, taking care to
avoid, if possible, having two lines of the same length;
and where the title can be measured as in the type it
may, the exact centre should be ascertained before
applying it heated on the gold. The back may now
be considered finished; the gold which has not been
impressed by the gilding tools must be well rubbed
off with the *gold rag*, and minutely cleared off with a
piece of fine flannel so as to display the delicate lines
of the ornaments as perfectly and clearly as possible.
Attention should be paid to this particular, for let a
book be finished in the most tasteful manner possible,
unless well cleared off, the effect is entirely lost. It
must now be polished, and the squares and edges of
the boards proceeded with.

GILDING THE SQUARES, &c.

For gilding the edges of the boards the gold may
be taken, as for the bands, on the roll, and the volume
held firmly with the left hand, but if large put into
the press between boards, so as not to injure the
back. Where the ornament of the square is simple,
the like proceeding of applying the gold will be pro-

per, resting the board open on an elevation equal to the thickness of the book. But if the square has been left large, with a leather joint, so as to admit of being more elaborately filled up, the gold must be laid on the whole space with the tip and pressed close with the cotton. The gilding is then proceeded with in the same manner, as will be fully detailed in the directions for the side ornaments.

GILDING THE SIDES.

The sides, from affording more ample space, are the part of the volume whereon the workman can, and is expected to, show his taste and skill in gilding. The proceedings are the same as before pointed out where a simple roll is the only ornament round, but where the pattern is extensive, and the details minute, it is necessary to have the whole worked dead upon the volume before glairing, and then apply the gold, If one side is done at a time, the book is taken by the leaves with the left hand, the board intended to be covered resting on the thumb, and the gold laid on as for the squares, either over the whole side, or on such parts as the pattern indicates. The gold may be laid on both boards by placing the leaves of the volume between two billets of wood, with the two boards resting flat upon their surface, as here sketched:

This affords greater facility for placing uniformly and

systematically the fillets, rolls, and tools necessary to complete the design on each side. Where the pattern has not been marked, and one side only proceeded with, the roll is run in a straight line, which should be made previous to covering with gold, on the board by the joint of the back, the volume turned for the head and tail, and laid open upon the board for the fore-edge to give it the firmness necessary. Directions for forming the most elaborate designs will be given under the head of Combination of Tools, whereby it will be perceived that it requires but taste, and a just observation of similarity of design, and the geometrical proportions of the ornaments, to execute them to any extent. One variation from this rule will destroy the effect of the whole pattern : it will therefore be to the benefit of such as are not conversant fully with the art, to assist themselves with designs drawn on cartridge paper, which may be marked through on the leather, and the pattern executed in gold or blind as required. In all, the gilding will be the same, either to glaire over the whole cover after the design is stamped, or if the plain part is to be left dull, by glairing the marks only with a camel's hair pencil.

If more extensive gilding is required, such as escutcheons, armouries, or large plates of flowers, vases, &c., for the centre of the volumes, or extensive corner-pieces, it will require the greatest attention to insure the proper execution of all the ornaments, so that every portion appear perfect. These pieces are

too large to be affixed by hand, and it is therefore
necessary to have recourse to the press. The difficulty, however, experienced in performing this part
of gilding properly in the common press, has led to
the invention of the arming-press described in the
section on tools, &c. But as this invention may not
be found available in some offices, where the business
is not extensive, the proceedings to be adopted with
the common press are here given. Having glaired
the parts and laid on the gold as before directed, the
volume must be opened and the board placed on a
thick billet of wood, fixed in the press, the rest of
the volume hanging in front; the engraved plate
heated to a degree that it is held in the hand with pain,
(if the cover is calf, if morocco, cooler), is then
placed on the board, paying every attention to its
being fixed perfectly straight, and in the exact spot
intended. The press must then be pulled strongly
and evenly down, and the impression will be given
immediately.

As nothing appears so ridiculous and disagreeable,
as a centre plate diverging from a right line to either
side, every precaution should be taken to prevent the
possibility of its doing so. To effect this the distances from each side of the border should be exactly
marked with the compasses, and lines slightly drawn
by the use of the square. The most simple plan, and
one that insures a certainty as to the centre of the
book, is to cut a piece of paper to the size of the
side, and fold it even both in the length and breadth.

The intersection of the lines being the exact centre, the arms or other ornament must be placed correctly on the paper, and an impression taken by means of the press. If correct, place the paper on the side of the book, put the block in the blind impression, and pull it through on the book. One coat of glaire pencilled in will here be sufficient for gilding. If the book has been cut true, the corner pieces cannot fail to be right if proper attention is paid. The proceedings to be adopted with the arming-press are the same as to the disposal of the book, but it will be advisable for the workman to study the description given, as also to turn to the directions for Blind Tooling, &c., where the subject will be further discussed.

It remains, however, here to speak of the gilt embellishments called embossed or Arabesque bindings. These are executed with designs cut in plates of brass the size of the sides of the book ; they were at first only used plain, but have latterly been adopted in gilding. Being cut to fit the board of the volume, the difficulty of placing the plate in a common press is not very great, but when performed with the arming press a precision is obtained that no other means can insure. This arises from the plate being affixed to the platten of the press, and descending sharply on the book, which is placed properly on the bed through the means of squares attached thereon. The gold must be fixed as before indicated, and after the impression is taken, rubbed well off so as to display the beauty of the design. The illuminated bindings pro-

perly come under this head, but from their importance they will be treated of in a separate section,
premising that, the further directions there given may
be useful in this place. The work, where required,
will now be ready for polishing.

GILDING ON SILK AND VELVET.

The proceedings necessary to be adopted for gilding on silk and velvet, are, from the delicate nature
of these substances, different from those laid down
for gilding on leather. The glaire used on the latter
would tend to stain, and therefore it is necessary to
employ other means for fixing the gold. This is by
drying the whites of eggs and reducing them to a
powder, which is put into a small bottle and tightly
tied over with a piece of fine muslin, by which means
it is equally distributed on the space intended to be
gilt. Gum Sandarac is now, however, more generally
used for this purpose. The powder being applied,
the gold is cut in slips and taken on a roll, of a cir-
cumference equal to the length of the space intended
for it to be applied on. The design is then firmly
impressed, and the superfluous gold brushed off with
a soft brush or clean piece of cotton, and the other
side alike executed. In lettering, or fixing single tools
on the back, the same proceedings must be adopted,
by taking the gold thereon and applying it to the back
or side of the volume. Where the design is large, or
elaborate work is required, it will be better executed in
the following manner. The design must be drawn on

paper, and worked through on the silk, after which the impression must be very carefully glaired with a camel's hair pencil ; when dry, rub the parts intended for the gold with the finger passed through the hair, or with a clean rag slightly oiled, and after laying on the gold as directed for other styles, reimpress the tools, and *whip* off the superfluous gold with a clean annel.

As there is no moisture in silk, the workman mus not lay on at one time so much as he does on calf and other substances.

ILLUMINATED BINDING.

This style, an invention of our neighbours, the French, and for some time by them kept with the greatest secresy, has been, after much expense, introduced into this country by Mr. Evans, book-binder, of Berwick Street, Soho, London. It is a binding of the utmost magnificence, uniting the varied beauties of the arabesque and gilt ornament, blended with the illuminated decorations seen on early MSS. before the invention of printing. When executed in the best manner, nothing can exceed the beauty of the whole *coup d'œil*, rivalling, as it does, in splen-dour, the most elaborately finished design of the painter. The time that requires to be devoted to the production of even one specimen, must ever confine this sort of ornament to the finest treasures of litera-ture, and even to them in a limited degree. Prac-tice, and a taste for the arts, will here alone serve the workman; without these requisites it would be futile to make the attempt. But as the proceedings require to be executed with the utmost care, we shall enter fully into such as are new, and, from their importance, at the risk of being considered prolix, again touch on those that may have been before treated of.

The description of one side will serve the purpose of making the proceedings fully understood. Whether the material be of morocco or white vellum, it must be washed, if required, perfectly clean, and left to dry. The first operation will be to place the side on the bed of the arming press, and boldly impress the design thereon. The most elegant and capable of the greatest display of colour, are subjects of botany and natural history. The next step will be to glaire with a camel's hair pencil such parts of the impression as it is intended shall be afterwards covered with gold. This done, the delicate operation of colouring may be proceeded with. In London and Paris this is executed by professed artists in no way conversant with bookbinding. The colours to be used must be such as do not at all, or very slightly fade, on exposure to the air or sun, such as carmine, ultramarine, indigo, burnt sienna, gamboge, and sap green. These must be prepared, with fine gum, in the same manner as for painting, and be as lightly and delicately laid on such parts of the design as it is intended the colour should occupy, taking care that the ground colour or leather is entirely hid. Let every thing be true to nature, each bird, plant, and flower its proper colou

L

and a general harmony prevail throughout. When finished, let the whole perfectly dry, and then, in the manner directed, lay gold on such parts as it is intended, in the re-impression of the plate, should be further embellished. Heat the plate, place the side again under it, and give it a firm and sharp impression. Rub off the superfluous gold, and the whole of the delicate lines of the ornament will be found beautifully gilt, the colours firmly fixed by the heat of the plate, and the rough edges of the colour completely effaced by the re-impression of the original design.

BLIND TOOLING.

This is an ornamental operation applied after the book has been gilt and polished, and if judiciously intermingled with the gold, will not fail to present a good effect. It is a style that has been much used of late years, and is executed in the same way and with the same tools as for gilding, but without any gold applied on the places thus ornamented. The rolls, pallets, and smaller tools are applied by the hand, and the large plates with the press, with the same precautions as indicated in the previous section. If the pattern consists of straight lines, and the workman possesses a good eye, the best manner of executing it is by making use of a pallet, placing it firmly on the book, and sliding it to the opposite point. It remains, therefore, to consider such matters as more immediately apply to this style of decoration.

The tools for blind tooling should not be so warm as for gilding, and particularly for morocco. If it is wished to be left dull, that is, free from glaire, the particles attaching themselves over the edge of the gold ornaments must be removed with the end of the finger, wrapped over with a piece of fine cloth, and wetted. This will soon wash it clean, and when dry the blind ornaments may be proceeded with.

Sometimes black fillets are applied upon morocco, or more frequently on rough calf. For this the tools are charged with black from the smoke of a candle, and affixed to the leather in the usual way. If a bolder impression only is required, a greater heat given to the tools will be sufficient.

Graining may be properly considered as a blind ornament. This is where, by the means of wooden or metal plates, the sides of a book are marked with lines crossed over each other, so as to form innumerable small squares in imitation of russia; or in imitation of the grain of morocco, scales of fish, and other substances. The operation is performed by placing the volume between the two plates even by the groove of the back, in the standing press, and pressing it tightly down, and so even that the plate will be impressed equally over the whole surface. Nothing will look worse than a bold impression in one place and a slight one in another, and therefore it becomes of importance to see that it is evenly pressed, as a second application of some kind of plates will never be found affixed to the same places.

ARABESQUE.

Arabesque ornaments have nearly superseded the
whole of the plates above spoken of, and we seldom
see any other than the cross or russia grain now
applied.   The arabesque, a description of binding
common in earlier times, was revived in France, and
introduced into this country in the year 1829, by Messrs.
Remnant and Edmonds, bookbinders, of Lovell's Court,
Paternoster Row, London.   It was first only adopted
in the binding of Bibles and Prayers, but soon carried to great extent in many other bindings, particularly of albums and books of illustration.   The
designs are imprinted on the leather by means of a
powerful arming press, and generally previous to its
being placed on the book, and at a rate of economy,
considering the richness of the ornaments and perfection of execution, almost incredible.   The covers in
morocco, roan, or other leather thus executed, may
be purchased at a price much below that for which
they could be produced on a limited scale; it will
therefore be to the advantage of the binder, if de-
sirous of executing binding in this style, to possess
himself of such as he may require.   The book to be
covered must always be cut to the exact size of the
design on the leather, carefully covered with glue so
as not to destroy the beauty of any part, and the lettering or other gilding proceeded with as before
directed.   The gilt arabesque will be the same as
before laid down under the section devoted to " Illu-

minated Bindings," omitting the colours. Any
pressing the book may require after covering must be
done between boards covered with five or six thicknesses of good flannel. It is not, however, usual to
place the better sort of bindings of this description
under the action of the press after covering.

COMBINATION OF TOOLS.

It is a subject of the utmost importance, in the
selection of tools for gilding, that the party have a
good knowledge of the style of binding peculiar to
the day, and a quick perception of the beauty of this
kind of ornament, the general bearing of the designs
towards each other, and their geometrical fitness for
application when combined, so as to produce a series
of patterns from the same tools. Without this, as
may be seen in many offices where judgment has not
presided in the selection, a large and expensive collection of tools may be provided, which cannot be
blended together without offence to the eye of taste,
from the defect presented in the complete design,
which even one unfit tool will cause. To assist the
binder in so important a point in Finishing as the
combination of tools, will be the object of this section
of the work; and it is hoped, that, if attention be
paid to the directions laid down, no one can fail,
with a well-selected assortment of good tools, to form
a very extensive series of scroll ornaments, flowers,
&c. The tools proper, his improved judgment will
teach him to select; and the examples, designed and

L 3

engraved for this work, from tools and ornaments
executed for this purpose alone, by Morris and Co.,
Engravers, Ludgate Street, London,* in illustration
of the subject, cannot fail to assist him in multiplying
the designs to an almost endless variety.

Plate I. is a representation of a small collection of
tools, numbering from 1 to 25, with which, and a
few gouges and plain lines, the designs figured on the
other plates are formed.   These will be referred to
by the numbers affixed to them.

In plate II. are designs for two backs of books.
The first figure, which presents an appearance of
exceeding richness, is executed with one sole tool,
viz. No. 10, and a small gouge for the sides of the
lettering-piece.   The back is marked into five compartments, the exact size of the tool from point to
point, and the tool worked five times across the back,
so as to form the upper part of the square.   This
done, the volume must be turned, and the ornament
executed on the bottom of the square.   The sides
must in like manner be worked, and the gouges on
the side of the title-piece.   The design will then be
complete ; but the greatest care will be- required in
observing that the tool fits exactly at the corners, as
it may readily be perceived that, unless it does so,
the circle formed by the four applications of it, will

---

* It is but justice to here make mention of the spirit and enterprise
with which the above gentlemen have carried on this branch of their art
of late years. Their patterns now amount to nearly twenty thousand
numbers, including every variety of ornament required in the most extensive establishment.

2

Morris & Cᵒ. Engravers & Tool Cutters 35 Ludgate Sᵗ London.

3

Morris & C? Engravers & Tool Cutters, 35 Ludgate S? London.

present a disagreeable effect. To insure a certain precision in cases where the combination is difficult, it is better to work off the design blind, before preparing the book for gilding.

The other design is formed of three tools, the upper two of which are joined together, so as to form a space for the lettering, by a single line tool; the tools are numbers 13, 18, 19. The book should be marked for the lettering-piece, and the figure 18, at the head, guided by the line, as also number 13 underneath. The tail of the volume will be the proper guide for 19. These tools do not present any particular combination, but their introduction serves to illustrate this peculiar style, now much in fashion. It will be seen, that any one of the three would answer the same purpose, by being applied three times on the back, and the sides of the title finished off by a plain single line. Also, that, by altering the position of any of them, a number of designs might be obtained.

Plate III. presents a diversity of ornament, viz. a lettering-piece, or centre plate, and four corners of various styles.

The lettering-piece is composed of a number of tools, figured 11, 12, 14, 15, 16, 17, two gouges, and a three-quarter circle. As it is most important that it occupy the true position, inclining neither to the left nor to the right, the design must be drawn on a piece of paper, and pasted at two or more points on the back of the book, and the tools be worked through. After the paper is removed, if on calf, and a coloured title required, a piece of morocco, pared as thin as possible and slightly damped, must be laid on the back, and pressed down with the palm of the hand till the whole of the tooling shows through. Then take it off, cut the edges with scissors, pare it round, and paste it on. In this design the first tool proper to be placed will be number 12, and then 17, taking especial care that they are exactly in the centre. These done, the pair of ornaments, figured 16, must be impressed at the top, one on each side, as shown in the engraving, and in like manner the other pair, numbered 11, at the bottom. The gouge and circle on the sides, and under the urn at the top, must be added, and the open spaces filled up with figures 14 and 15, as seen in the design.

The corners will be worked true, provided the boards have been cut perfectly square, but to insure a greater precision, it will be preferable to work them on a triangular piece of paper, and prick the points through on the book. The first corner at the head of the plate is formed from figures 1, 2, and 4, and three or four gouges and circles. The circular corner is first worked, then the first pair of scrolls, one on each side. Each scroll is farther lengthened by the addition of figures 2 and 4. The plain gouges inside are then worked at parallel distance from the others, and the corners joined to each other by a plain fillet.

4

Morris & Cᵒ Tool Cutters & Engravers 34 Ludgate Sᵗ London.

The other corner at top is composed of line tools only, and worked in a similar manner to the above.

Figures 4, 8, and 9, with two small gouges, are only necessary to form the first corner at the foot of the plate. The larger gouge being worked on each angle from the corner, figure 8 must then be applied, one on each side, and then, branching onwards, figures 9 and 4. The large gouge is then again worked twice in the centre, parallel with the scrolls, and once a little more advanced, adding a smaller gouge to it twice, as seen in the design. This gouge is also worked once near the corner, connecting the two large scrolls.

The last corner is of a more ornamented description, and formed of figures 3, 5, 6, and 7 To insure its occupying the exact position, if not previously worked on paper, a line should be marked from the corner towards the middle of the book, at equal distances from the two angles of the sides. Figure 3, will be the first to be worked off, and be then joined by number 6, both occupying the centre of the line. The side ornaments, number 5, must then be added, one on each side, and finished by the small scrolls 7.

In Plate IV. we have the figure of a book open, showing the back and front side of it. The back is ornamented by numbers 22 and 23, the latter being worked double in the middle. As shown before, these tools would make several different patterns. The design round the side is formed by the union of four

tools, 4, 20, 21, and 24, with two small gouges and a
plain line. Being marked as before directed, figure
21 is impressed in all the corners, and lengthened out
with the plain line to the point where number 20
joins. One of the scrolls, 24, is then worked in the
angle of the corner tool, and the other in the opposite
angle. These are then repeated in such way that the
end or point joins the one first put on, and the whole
terminated by figure 4. The two gouges are then
worked in parallel lines with the scrolls, and the whole
finished by placing number 20 at the angles, to form
the interior square. The lines connecting the designs
at the corners, and forming the square, are executed
with a plain fillet, taking care that it does not disfigure the other ornament by extending over. The
centre piece is composed of number 25, and some of
the gouges worked up in the designs before described.
The middle of the square will be ascertained by folding a piece of paper, as directed for the arms, and in
this case working the design and pricking it through
on the book. The small square being formed, by
working the gouge four times, figure 25 must be
placed on, twice each; the four points must then be
executed by working the gouge eight times. After
this, the design is completed by working the half circles inside, and by the addition outside of the half
circle eight times and three-quarter circle twice, as
shown in the engraving.

The examples given will be sufficient for the intellectual workman to conceive many patterns which his taste will suggest, forming an infinite variety of beautiful designs. In all combinations, a rigorous observance of the symmetrical proportions of the tools must be his first care, so that the union of any number of designs present a form agreeable and chaste. It would be superfluous to add more ; but from the importance of the subject, on closing the directions for the ornamental department of binding, it may be repeated, that there is no greater evidence of the ignorance or carelessness of the workman, than an ornament of any kind unevenly or unequally worked. Let the young binder especially bear this in mind : it is a defect which nothing can effectually remedy ; instead of an embellishment, it is a detriment to the binding, and his reputation as a clever workman is consequently placed in jeopardy.

In many designs, the corner pieces are combined so as to form the centre ornament on the sides of books. This, however, takes a considerable time in the execution, the tool having to be applied eight times on each side. For greater expedition in working this style of ornament, Mr. Bain, of Broad Court, Long Acre, has contrived an ingenious method, for which invention he was presented with the silver Isis medal, and five pounds, by the Society of Arts.

The economy is effected by employing four triangular *blocks*, capable of being fixed in a simple adjustable frame, so as to suit the size of any book. The frame on the left holds the rods parallel to each

other, having a groove for them to be set at any required distance. The blocks are perforated to slide
on the rods, and are fixed to their positions by small
set screws at their back, which bind upon the rods.
The small screws at the ends of the rods are to prevent the blocks falling off before they are adjusted.
The following sketch represents the whole arrangement.

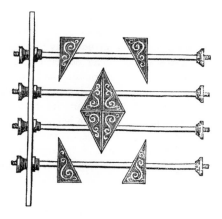

When the corners are done, if the same ornament is
intended for the centre, they may be transposed on
the rods, and the work executed, but it will save time
to have blocks for both, as the ornament will be more
uniform, and a certainty of being placed in the centre
insured. The impression is given by placing the
book and design in the standing press.

POLISHING.

The details of this operation, which is performed immediately after the gold ornaments have been worked, has been reserved for the last section of Part II., in order that the whole of the ornamental department might be kept together. Morocco, roan, silk, and velvet, and the blind ornaments on any substance, must never be submitted to the action of the polisher. A smart rubbing with a piece of rough calf will be sufficient for the two former, and the velvet or silk will merely require cleaning with any smooth substance, or with India-rubber.

There are two polishers, one for the back and bands, and another for the sides, both of which will be described in the Chapter on Tools. The oil applied on the cover previous to laying on the gold will be sufficient to make the polisher glide easily over the surface. The polisher must be heated, and well cleaned on a board, and passed quickly and evenly on the back, sides, or joints, as the case may be, taking especial care that it is not too hot, as the glaire would thereby be turned white, and the work damaged in appearance, nor so cold as to give a bad polish.

The book, as gilt, must be first polished on the back, by taking it with the left hand and applying the other end against the stomach, and polished with the right hand by gliding backwards and forwards the smooth part of the polisher on the whole

M

extent of the back.   Should bands have been placed, it will be necessary to apply the polished corner of the iron on each side, ranging across the back.   This not only polishes the surface, but smooths down the indentations formed upon the leather by the gilding-tools, bringing up the gilding to the surface.   The polisher must be passed on such places only as it is wished to make brilliant, and great care taken not to touch the places intended to be left dull.

The sides are similarly polished, by laying the volume on the table, covered with baize, and passing the large iron quickly over, first from the fore-edge towards the groove, and then, by turning the volume in a contrary way, from the tail to the head.

If the joint requires polishing, the book is laid before the workman, the tail towards him, and the iron applied on the side next the groove, polishing the whole length of the board; then turning round the volume, and bringing the gutter towards him, he polishes the side on the fore-edge, and turning again, completes the whole by polishing the parts at the head and tail, applying the iron very forcibly on the corners to reduce their thickness.

In addition to polishing, it is deemed desirable to give to the sides the greatest possible smoothness by pressing them between polished tins or horns.   These are placed on each side of the book even by the groove, put between pressing boards, and screwed tightly in the press, and left for some time.   In conclusion, we here give two receipts for

VARNISH,

as used in bookbinding. The first, by the celebrated *Tingry*, will be found the most available in practice, and the best composition as yet known, from its brilliant and drying qualities.

Put into a vessel six ounces of mastic, in drops, three ounces of sandarac finely powdered, four ounces of coarsely-broken glass, separated from the dust by a sieve, and thirty-two ounces of spirit of wine, of about forty degrees ; place the vessel upon straw in another filled with cold water ; put it on the fire and let it boil, stirring the substances together with a stick, to keep the resins from uniting. When the whole appears well mixed, put in three ounces of turpentine, and boil for another half-hour, when the whole must be taken off and stirred till the varnish and the water in which it is placed cools. Next day, filter it through a fine cotton, by which means it will acquire the greatest degree of limpidity, and well cork up in a bottle.

The other receipt is given by *Mons. F. Mairet* of *Chatillon sur Seine*, and may be prepared similar to the above. The ingredients are, three pints of spirits of wine, of thirty-six to forty degrees, eight ounces of sandarac, two ounces of mastic in drops, eight ounces of shell-lac, and two ounces of Venice turpentine.

The varnish is first put on the back of the book with a camel's-hair brush as lightly as possible. When nearly dry, it is polished with a ball formed of fine white cotton, filled with wool, on which has been rubbed a small quantity of olive oil, to make it glide freely; it must be rubbed at first lightly, and as fast as the varnish dries and becomes warm, more sharply. The sides are in like manner polished one after the other.

Varnish is applied more particularly on black coloured books, or such as have not been polished with the iron, but may be used on any books when found not sufficiently brilliant. In the latter case, the volume should be perfectly dry, or the varnish will not take. The application of this composition has also the effect of preserving the covers from some accidents damp is likely to occasion.

PART III.

OF STATIONERY, OR VELLUM BINDING.

THIS branch of the art of Bookbinding, in large towns, is a distinct business, and presents some difference in the mode of proceeding in several of the manipulations required. These, as in previous parts of the work, will be minutely entered into for the instruction of the young workman, whilst those which are executed in the same manner as directed for printed books, will be merely referred to in the order they will be required to be executed.

Stationery binding includes every description of paper book, from the *Memorandum*, which is simply covered with marble paper, to the most firm and elaborate bound book used in the counting-house of the merchant and banker. Of the more simple and common bindings, it will not be necessary to enter into minute details, the proceedings being the same as for others, only omitting the more expensive operations, the price allowed making it necessary to bind them in a more simple manner. The first proceeding, should the work require it, will be the

RULING.

This is done by a machine or by the hand. An

M 3

engraving of the ruling machine will be found in the fifth part of the work. Where an office possesses one, after the pens are adjusted to the proper pattern, the work will be speedily accomplished, and an uniformity presented that no hand ruling can effect. The description given with the engraving will fully explain the mode of operation. When once set to the pattern, and the pens properly cleaned by running a piece of thin brass latten through them, it will only be necessary to keep up an equal supply of ink, to see that each line is clearly marked, and that the double ones do not run blind.

As it would not be found advisable to introduce a ruling machine where this description of work is limited, it may be requisite to give particulars relative to hand ruling, which will be found necessary to execute in every office, premising only that the laying open the paper for both will be the same. The paper, which generally is procured from the wholesale stationers ruled with blue lines, unless previously done, must be opened out by breaking the back of the fold, and refolded evenly in small sections. The pattern for the red lines being placed in front, the whole must be knocked evenly up at the back and head, put between boards, the top of the paper projecting, and screwed in the laying-press. Then with the saw let the marks of the red ink on the pattern be sawn across the whole, which will denote the places for the lines on the right-hand side pages throughout the book. In like manner, placing the pattern on the other side, and sawing the bottom of the paper, will the marks of the left-hand pages be denoted. Care must be taken to leave a larger space on the fore-edge to allow for cutting. Should a head line be required, it must be similarly marked on the fore-edge of the paper. This done, re-open the whole of the sections, and, with a round ruler and tin pen, proceed to rule the whole of the head lines on one side of the paper. This, as well as every division of £. *s. d.* or other distinct column, must be ruled double, as close as possible, taking care that both are distinct, and that they do not run into each other. The headline being completed on one side, turn the whole of the paper, and operate in like manner on the other. Then turning the paper, so as to have the head lines to the left, proceed to rule the columns marked for the *date, amount,* &c., taking especial care that the pen always commences by the line at the head, and that it never entrenches on the space above, which would disfigure the work. As for the head line, so here the whole of one side of the paper must be completed before the other is commenced, attention being paid to each line being perpendicular, clear, and as even in colour as possible.

INKS.

To give to the work the best effect, it will be necessary to be provided with good inks, and it being connected with the subject, some receipts for their preparation are subjoined.

RED.

Half a pound of Brazil dust, half an ounce of cochineal, a little alum, and four quarts of vinegar. Let them steep for twelve hours, then strain for use.

ANOTHER.

Boil in a quart of soft water a quarter of a pound of Brazil dust; when boiled, put in one ounce of ground alum, one ounce of white stone crystal, and boil for three minutes, and strain.

BLUE.

The *liquid blue* at page 78, mixed with water to the shade desired, will be found to answer every purpose. But as this liquid, if used in the manufactured state, will, what is termed, *run* on the paper, it will be necessary to kill the spirit contained in it previous to using, which is done as follows :—

Put four ounces of ground alum in a bason, and two ounces of salts of tartar in another; then pour on each two pints of boiling water and let them stand for one hour, when add the two together, and they will bubble as if boiling, and turn white. After remaining two hours, tie a cloth round the bason and let the water run off gradually. Pour over the sediment remaining a kettle full of boiling water; let it then remain until dry, when cut it into small pieces, and put them to the *liquid blue*. After remaining two or three days, the spirit will be wholly out. Common chalk is by some considered equally effective.

BLACK.

Half a pound of nutgalls, a quarter of a pound of sulphate of zinc (white vitriol), two ounces of gum arabic, and a handful of salt. Boil the nutgalls half an hour in three quarts of soft water, then put the whole together, and let stand for use.

ANOTHER.

For making a larger quantity, put in ten gallons of rain water, five pounds and a quarter of nutgalls, well bruised, one pound and a half of logwood chips, the like quantity of copperas, and a quarter of a pound of alum. Let them stand a few days, and then add two ounces of gum arabic and an ounce and a half of verdigris. Stir them all well together two or three times a day for a fortnight or three weeks, and the ink will then be fit for use.

FOLDING.

The whole being ruled, it will be proper to fold the book to the size required into sections for sewing. The number of leaves in each must depend on the thickness of the paper and size of the book, taking care that there are not so many as when cut, to cause the leaves to start, or so few that the backs will be swollen too much by the thread. Then place the whole evenly in the standing-press for some time, and prepare the end papers, which must be of blank paper, and outsides, unless the work is of a superior

description. Should leather or cloth joints be placed,
it will be necessary to sew them on with the end
papers, as before directed.

SEWING.

The sewing of stationery differs much from that of
printed books. To allow of the greatest possible
strength, elasticity, and freedom, they are sewn on
slips of vellum without being marked with the saw,
and the whole length of each sheet, with waxed
thread. For small books, two slips will be sufficient;
for foolscap folio, three will be required ; and where
larger, the number must be increased, according to
the length of the back, leaving a space of about two
inches between each. The plan laid down by *M.
Lesne,* page 21, might, perhaps, be adopted here with
fine and light work to great advantage. The slips
should be cut about an inch wide, and of sufficient
length to extend about an inch over each side of the
back. This portion being bent down at one end of
the slips, they must be placed under the end-paper on
the table, at such places as may be deemed proper,
and the section sewn the whole length ; and so fol-
lowed by every portion till the whole are attached in
the same manner, taking care that the slips retain a
perpendicular position, and that the back be not too
much swollen. Should a morocco joint have been
inserted, it must be sewn on with strong silk of the
same colour. When finished, the coloured end-papers,
if any, must be pasted in, and the first and last ruled

leaves similarly attached to the end-papers. If joints, the same precautions must be adopted as before directed. The book may then be beat even on the back and head, placed again in the laying-press, and glued up, working the brush well on the back, so as to force the glue between the sections.

CUTTING.

When the ends and back are dry, this will be the next operation. Here the fore-edge must be cut first. It is done before altering the form of the book, but exactly as in printed works, paying great attention to the knife running evenly across, so that the column nearest the front is not cut too close, and is parallel to the edge. When taken out, the back must be rounded with the hammer, in a greater degree than for other bindings, and placed again evenly in the standing press. After remaining a short time the head and tail must in like manner be cut, but offer no difference in operation. The book will now be ready for colouring the edges ; all the proceedings for sprinkling are the same as at page 31, but as the marbling is of a distinct character, it will now be detailed at length. The kind used in stationery binding is called

DUTCH MARBLE.

The *colours* used are the same as for other marbles, and ground up with the wax in a similar manner. The size and preparations of the colours, &c., are,

however, different, and therefore require to be minutely
described.

The Size.—Put in any vessel half a pail of soft
water, and dissolve therein three ounces of gum dra-
gon, stirring it from time to time for two or three
days till the whole obtains a consistence strong enough
to support the colours, and prevent their mixing with
it. It should be made stronger than necessary to
use, so that any portion that may have been weakened
too much in the trough by the addition of water, may
be readily strengthened by more gum.

The Gall.—To the gall of an ox add eighteen grains
of camphor dissolved in twenty-five grains of spirit of
wine, and beat the whole well together. This preparation should not be made long before it may be
required, as it will not keep.

Preparation of the Colours.—As for other marbles,
a portion of each colour must be put in separate cups;
they must then be well mixed up to a proper consistence with the prepared gall, and trial made on
a *small portion* of the size. If they extend too
much, more colour must be added; if not sufficiently, a further portion of the gall. By this
means, too, trials of the strength of the size will be
made. This is done by agitating the colour with a
pointed stick. If it extends itself, and forms the vo-
lute well without mixing with the size, it is strong
enough; but if the colour does not turn easily in the
direction of the stick, it is too strong, and will then
require water to be added and well beat up. If, how-

ever, the colour extends too much, or mixes with the size, it will require more of the reserved size to be added, and well mixed together. At each trial thus made, the *portion* used should be thrown away, and fresh taken. When the size is ascertained to be of the proper consistence, it should be poured into the trough, about an inch in height, and the marbling proceeded with.

Clear off the top of the size with a piece of waste paper, and having prepared the colours as above directed, proceed to lay them on. For this description of marble, instead of brushes, the colours must be conveyed to the places desired with quills or iron pencils. For example, suppose the marble to be formed of four colours, red, orange, blue, and green : the red is drawn across the size in various places, then the blue between, and afterwards the orange and green in the spaces between the first two, in such manner that the whole surface of the size is completely covered. Then taking the *comb*, draw it across in a contrary direction, that is from left to right, so that the colours run into each other in a jagged form. Let this be done in various places, and then in the spaces left in like manner from right to left, till the whole assumes one body of diversified forms. Then taking the book, dip in this case the fore-edge first, and with the precautions directed for the other marbles. After clearing off the refuse colour, proceed in the same way with the head and tail, and leave the edge to dry.

N

Marbles with volutes, or any other fancy design, may be formed with a pointed stick and proceeded with in the manner directed above. Further detail will not be necessary, but it may be advisable to direct attention to the instructions laid down at page 37.

BOARDING.

The next operation will be the preparation of the boards for the side covers, which should be formed of two or three thin milled boards pasted together. These must be cut to the proper size with the plough, so as to leave a perfectly even edge, and will require to have a larger square allowed for than usual in printed books. When cut they must be pasted together, leaving, if the book is heavy and the slips on which it is sewn thick, a space at the back to place them in. The book must now be headbanded, and then it will be proper to strengthen the back of the book by glueing across, on the spaces between the slips, strong pieces of canvass, and at the head and tail a piece of calf, leaving projections on each side to be attached to the board. For additional firmness, it is usual, where the work is of a superior description, to sew the length of the book with catgut in about ten or fourteen places, according to the thickness. This is done by placing three slips of strong leather in spaces between the vellum ones, and sewing as at first, by which means the gut crossing over the leather and under the vellum slips on the back, appears inside on the spaces where no thread has before passed.

For ornament, another thread is twisted round the gut on the back, so as to present the appearance of a double cord. These matters being adjusted, the slips of calf at the head and tail must be let in by cutting the end of the waste leaf and placing them under. The other slips, of every description, after trimming, must then be put into the space left between the boards, which should be previously well pasted or glued, the boards placed nearly half an inch from the back, and perfectly square on the sides, and the whole screwed tightly in the standing press for some time.

THE SPRING BACK.

There are numerous ways of forming this description of back, and as generally adopted in different offices. As in other particulars, two or three of the best will here be given. 1 —Having ascertained the width and length of the back, and provided a piece of strong pasteboard, or thin milled board, of little more than twice the width, fold one side rather more than half, and then the other, so that the middle space left will be the exact size required, which should be about a quarter of an inch wider than the back of the book : then cut evenly another piece, a little less than the width, then another still less, and so on for six or seven, lessening the width each time till the last is merely a narrow slip. Let the edges of the first, or cover for the whole, be pared, and laid open on the table ; then glue the middle

N 2

space, and place thereon the largest slip, which also
glue, and add the next in size, proceeding in like
manner till the smallest is fixed, taking especial care
that each occupies the exact centre of the one on
which it is placed. Finally, glue the whole space
and the two side slips of the first, which must be
brought over and firmly rubbed down. Shape it to
the curve of the back of the book, either on the back
or a wooden roller of the same size, and leave it to
dry, when the head and tail must be cut to the proper
length with the shears. For greater security the
whole is often covered with linen cloth.

2. Cut a piece of firm milled board to the size
required, and pare down the edges; then hold the
board to the fire till it is found soft enough to model
almost into any shape, and form to the back as above
directed. The board is sometimes wetted, but does
not answer so well.

3. A beaten iron plate of the exact size, and
covered with parchment or leather.

Numerous patents have been obtained for this description of back. Among the earliest were those
taken out by Messrs. Palmer and Williams, which
have been long disused, as they were found to break
from falls and other accidents. The specification
delivered in by Mr. Palmer, in 1800, is here given,
as an illustration of the early attempts made to improve this kind of binding :—

" There are certain various small bars of metal, or
composition of metals, about the thickness of a

shilling or more, according to the size and thickness of the book to be made, the length of each such
bar being from half an inch to several inches long, in
proportion to the strength required in the back of the
book.

" At each end of every such bar of metal is made a
pivot, by being filed down or otherwise, and which
are of different lengths, also in proportion to the
thickness of two links, which they are to receive.

"There are a certain number of links, made rather
in an oval form, to the said hinge, each of which contains two holes, according to the size of the pivots
they are to go on, which links are of the same metal
as the hinge, or a composition of metals, as is judged
necessary; each of the said links being nearly the
length that two of the above-described bars are
wide.

" When such metallic pivots are prepared, the
aforesaid links are then rivetted on those pivots, each
pivot receiving two links, and thereby holding the
said hinge together, on the principle of a link chain
or hinge.

"There are two holes, or more, of different sizes,
as required on each bar of the hinge or chain, by
which means each section of the book is strongly
fastened to the same; which hinge so fastened ope-
rates with the back of the book, when bound in such
an improved manner, that thereby occasions the
said section to open in, so as to bring them on a
parallel with each other, and in consequence thereof

admit of the ruled lines being written into, even close
to the back without any inconvenience."

The spring back is only used for the superior kind
of account books ; for common work, a piece of thin
pasteboard is merely laid on the back before covering,
the stress on the back being small.

To prevent the manufactured back slipping during
the operation of covering, it is laid on, and a piece
of cloth glued over and attached to the sides, similarly to the back of a half-bound book. This tends
also to materially strengthen the back.

COVERING.

The materials generally used for stationery binding
are russia, rough calf, green and white vellum, and
forrel, according to the value of the work.   Previous
to pasting on vellum and forrel, the book should be
covered with a piece of strong paper, as if for boards.
The process is the same as for other bindings; but
when completed, it will be necessary to put the book
in the standing press, having pieces of cane or wood
for the purpose placed between the boards and the
back, so as to form a bold groove, and force the leather close on the edge of the spring back.   Previous
to and after pressing, the headbands must be squarely
set, taking care to rub out any wrinkles that may
have been formed in turning in the cover.   Should
the book be very large, it may be advisable to give
it a nip in the press immediately after folding in the

fore-edges of the boards, and then finish the covering by turning in the head and tail.

As circumstances, such as the fancy of some previous workman, or coloured vellum not to be obtained so early as required, may make it necessary to execute the proper colours, the proceedings are here given.

GREEN.

Put one ounce of verdigris and one ounce of white wine vinegar into a bottle, and place them near the fire for five days, shaking it three or four times each day. Wash the vellum over with weak pearl-ash, and then colour it to the shade desired.

RED.

To one pint of white wine vinegar, put a quarter of a pound of Brazil dust and a piece of alum. Cork the mixture up; let it stand in a warm place for two or three days.

PURPLE.

Proceed as for the *red*, substituting logwood chips for the Brazil dust.

YELLOW.

Half an ounce of turmeric to half a pint of spirits of wine, prepared as above.

BLACK.

Wash the vellum over three times with the red, nd whilst wet, colour with strong marbling ink.

Marbles and other designs may be formed on white vellum, but as the proceedings have been so fully entered into before, it will not be necessary here to repeat them. Where russia bands are not added, the end-papers must now be pasted down, and the lettering, &c. proceeded with. If bands are attached, the pasting down of the end-papers and joints must be deferred till they are executed.

RUSSIA BANDS.

To give to large books the greatest possible degree of strength, it is usual to affix russia bands to them. They are called *single* when they extend about half way down the sides, and *double* when those at the head and tail reach to the corners of the boards, and are turned over the edges in the same manner as the cover. For *single*;—having ascertained the breadth by dividing the back with the compasses into *seven* spaces, cut three pieces of russia perfectly square and the exact size of the spaces they are to occupy, and paste them on the *second, fourth,* and *sixth* division of the back, thereby leaving in sight the first, third, fifth, and seventh spaces with the cover only; draw them squarely on the sides, and place the volume in the press, with the rods fixed to force the russia into the joints as before directed, and then leave to dry. Where *double* bands are to be placed on a book, divide the back into five spaces, or seven, if four bands. The middle band or bands will be short like those above, and placed on in the same manner ; but those at the head and tail, which extend their whole length, to the fore-edge of the boards, will require paring on the edge intended to be turned in at the headbands and over the boards of the book, cutting the corners and squaring the edges, as in covering. When done, press the whole, with the rods as before, to cause the russia to adhere well and evenly to the vellum or calf, and leave it to dry. The next proceeding will be to mark the places for the holes intended to lace in the white vellum thongs on the bands ; this done, the holes must be pierced with the bodkin, and the vellum passed through, crossing each other so as to form diamonds, squares, or other forms, as taste may direct. All being executed, by every part being evenly laid and tightly drawn, the thongs must be fastened inside, and well beat down with the backing hammer. When the end-papers are pasted, tins must invariably be placed inside during pressing, to prevent the impression of the lacing-slips on the leaves of the book.

CLASPS, CORNERS, AND BRASS BANDS.

Clasps are generally affixed to the better kind of stationery books, as keeping them closed when not in use, tends much towards their preservation. And for still greater security, they are often further pro-

tected with brass corners or bands. To hide the projection the clasps would make on the fore-edge, that
part of the board must be cut away to admit the clasp,
so that when fixed it will be even with the edge of
the board. For the corners and bands this is not
done ; but to insure a finished appearance in the
whole, the workman's attention must be directed to
their fitting exactly in every particular of length,
breadth, and thickness. The clasps may be purchased
of the makers, but it may be found necessary to place
the making of the bands and corners in the hands of
the brass-worker, to whom particular directions and
sizes must be given. They must fit tightly to the
boards, run exactly parallel with the edges, and have
the holes for the rivets drilled through previously to
placing on. Where corners are put on, no bands
will be required. Bands which extend from the
back to the fore-edge and form a corner equal to the
breadth of the band, being squarely soldered in front,
are placed at the head and tail of the book, and
fastened with rivets in the following manner, as are
also the clasps and corners. Pierce the boards with
a fine bodkin in such places as are previously drilled
in the brass, and force through brass rivets of a
length sufficient to project about the eighth of an
inch, and with heads made to fit exactly to the cavi-
ties formed in the bands ; then fasten them firmly,
by placing the heads of each on an iron, and beating
down with a hammer the part projecting inside, till it
is smooth and even with the surface. Bosses, which

are seen fixed on the middle of the boards of old books, particularly of early-bound Bibles, &c., in churches, are fastened in the same manner. These, however, are now almost entirely disused.

FINISHING.

The placing of lettering-pieces, gilding, and blind tooling, is exactly the same as for printed books. Rough calf must be dressed with pummice-stone, cleaned with a brush, and ornamented blind, with the tools very hot, to form a dark impression. Vellum will require the tools cooler than calf. The book now being ready for the use of the accountant, necessarily closes the details of this description of binding.

PART IV.

OF BOARDING.

In London and other large places, this is another distinct branch of the art, and consists of simply covering the book with coloured paper, or other common substance. In small towns, it must necessarily be executed jointly with the other branches; but so ample and minute has been the detail of the various manipulations in a previous part of this work, that in attempting a description of BOARDING, little can be said without repetition. This style, too, being the commonest mode of doing up books in this country, also places the subject, under any circumstances, in a position requiring but little remark. Previous, therefore, to speaking of the few processes that are peculiar to boarding, it will only be necessary to observe, that the folding, pressing, sewing, backing, boarding, covering, and pasting down, are the same as for regularly bound books. It remains, then, to add, that the books will not require beating, and, for common boards, are never cut round the edges. The leaves are only dressed with the trimming-knife previous to rounding the back, so as to present as neat an appearance as possible, by removing every portion of paper projecting over the general line. For greater strength to the back, a piece of paper must be pasted in the centre of the coloured paper previous to applying it on the volume. When covered and pasted down, the printed label must be fixed evenly on the back, and the book will be finished.

CLOTH BOARDING,

Now so extensively adopted, offers nothing new for remark in the early operations, except that the covers are put on the boards with glue, as paste would tend to destroy the gloss on the cloth, by the damp striking through it. Where a great number of one work (which on first publication is generally the case) are executed at one time, it is usual to prepare the covers before placing them on the volume, by cutting the boards to the proper size with the plough, and covering them with cloth. A piece of stiff pasteboard, of the width of the back, must be placed between the boards, which should be at a distance from each other equal to the breadth of the back and the allowance for the joints. This board must also be covered with the cloth at the head and tail, and when the case is applied to the volume, will form an open back. This mode is called CASE-WORK, and executed as follows :—Back the volume, and cut off the bands or slips on which it has been sewn; then place it in the cover by pasting the guards (small slips of paper), left over the end-papers, which an-

o

swers the purpose of lacing. There are some other operations which it will be necessary to describe more particularly.

EMBOSSING AND LETTERING.

This has been carried to great perfection on cloth, being executed with the *arming press* with ease and quickness. The front boards, or upper part of the backs, as the case may be, are rubbed slightly with oil, and the gold laid on; when, the squares on the bed of the press being adjusted to the right position, the lettering is executed as swiftly as they can be laid on and removed. If the boards have been laced in, the sides only can be lettered, by placing the whole volume on the press, the board laying open and flat on the bed; but if the cases are previously made, the lettering, &c., must be executed on the back or sides previous to fixing on the book. The size in the cloth, as now manufactured, will be sufficient to hold firmly the gold when stamped with the heated design. The portion not thus marked must be removed with the gold-rag, and rubbed clear with a piece of fine woollen-cloth. When lettered, it will remain only to paste down the end-papers, and the book will be completed. Embossed ornaments may be placed blind in a similar manner with the arming-press.

PART V.

ON MACHINES, PRESSES, TOOLS, &c.

In describing the various manipulations in binding a book, it has frequently been necessary to refer
to the presses, machines, and tools requisite for their
proper execution. Skilled and proficient as the
binder may be, and however good the material he
may have for use, unless he is aided by good presses
and well-executed tools, his work will not present
some of those important qualities of good binding
laid down in previous parts of this treatise, viz. solidity in the forwarding, and true proportion in the
finishing. In fitting up an office, it becomes therefore necessary for the proper execution of the work,
and the consequent reputation of the binder, that
he provide himself with machinery, &c. of the best
manufacture only. True it is, that the cost may be
greater, but assuredly it will soon be amply repaid by
the increased effect produced, and the consequent
satisfaction which superior workmanship will always
give to the possessor of a library. But, with judgment, a greater cost need not be incurred, for, as has
been before observed, the binder may be enabled to
purchase the necessary and most approved articles for

his establishment for a smaller sum than, without
calculation and reflection, he would expend in pro-
curing those of an inferior description.   The fitness
of the articles for the extent of business to which
they are to be applied must be the primary consideration, and to enable him to judge which will be most
applicable, as well as being a necessary portion of the
work, will be the object of the present section,
wherein will be given a detailed account of the most
important presses and tools, and a description of
every other article used in the art of bookbinding.
For more ready reference, the subject will be divided
into three classes, viz. presses and machines, tools
used in forwarding, and tools required by the finisher.

PRESSES AND MACHINES.

The most important are the presses used for com-
pressing the sheets of a book as much as possible,
so as to give the whole the greatest firmness.   The
most generally adopted is the

COMMON STANDING PRESS.

This consists of two upright cheeks of timber, of
about seven feet in height, placed at a distance of
from two to three feet from each other.   At about
six inches from the bottom, the bed, formed of a
solid piece of wood, is let in by means of grooves between the cheeks ; and, at the like distance from the
top, another to form the head. in which is placed the

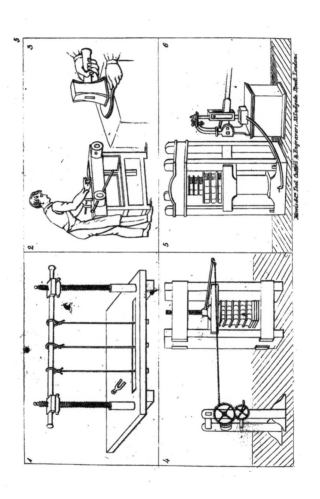

Morris &Co. Tool Cutters &Engravers, Aldersgate Street London.

box for the screw. The bed is about four inches and the head twelve inches in thickness. The screw was formerly made of wood, but the greater pressure acquired from the use of a well-turned iron thread, has caused the use of wood to be nearly discarded altogether. To this screw is affixed the swinging board, which works perpendicularly between the bed and the head of the press, and is raised or lowered by turning the screw in the box, by means of a small iron bar. To give to the press all the force possible, it is pulled tightly down with a large iron bar, five or six feet in length, and to which the united strength of two or more men will be required when the press is full. A winch is sometimes applied, to give additional force. Figure 4, in the annexed engraving, will tend to make these particulars fully understood.

THE ATHOL STANDING PRESS.

This press, which is represented in the engraving, number VI., is an improvement on the common press, from the greater power of compression it possesses. It is formed of four upright cheeks of six-inch cast iron, having a bed and head similar to the one above described. The screw is generally four and a half inches diameter, and worked in a gun-metal box by means of a cog-wheel and worm of Athol power. The great advantage in this press, in addition to its great pressure, is the small space in which it can be worked. No lever or windlass being required, the smallest space over that which the

press occupies, will be necessary for the application
of the force. It will not recede if left for any time,
and possesses the further recommendation, that the
concussion to the walls, floors, &c. occasioned by the
jerk of the bar in the common press, is entirely pre-
vented, as well as the damage the box in the head of
the press is liable to sustain.   A larger press on the
same principle is manufactured, which is employed in
the pressing of paper.   This press is the invention
of Mr. Hopkinson, of New North Street, Finsbury,
London.

THE HYDRAULIC PRESS,

Which forms figure 6 in plate V., is the most powerful of any yet invented. It is manufactured by
nearly all the press-makers, differing only in the
general design, the application of the power being
the same.   The one shown in the plate is taken from
that of Messrs. Cope and Sherwin, and by applying
the water power to the *Athol*, with four cast iron
cheeks, as before described, a just conception may be
formed of that made by Mr. Hopkinson.   The general
outline of the press, it will be seen, is the same, but
the application of the power from below, instead of
above, as in the common and Athol presses.   The
power of compression is derived from the pump to
the right of the press, which is supplied with water
from a cistern sunk under it.   The water thus sent
by means of the tube seen passing from it to the centre of the foot of the press, causes the cylinder to

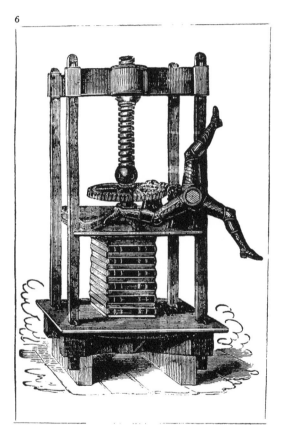

which the bed is fixed to rise and compress the books or paper tightly between the bed and head of the press. When it is forced as high as can be by means of the pump-handle seen, a larger bar is attached, and worked by two men. The extraordinary power of this press is so great, as to cause, particularly in common work, a saving of more than three-fourths of the time required in bringing books to a proper solidity by the common press. When it is wished to withdraw the books, the small cock at the end of the tube at the foot of the press is turned, the water flows into the cistern below, and the bed with the books glides gently down in front of the workman. Two presses are frequently worked by the same pump, one being on each side.

BARNES' STANDING PRESS.

This is a new invention from America, and will be fully understood by the following report of the Committee on Science and the Arts of the Franklin Institute, to whom the press was referred for examination :—

"This press embraces the following combination of simple machines, viz. a single screw in the centre of a cast iron frame, moving vertically through a nut or box in the upper part of the said frame, which box is supported, when the press is not in use, on a cross plate below, and when in action is kept down by the upper head of the frame. To the box is attached a toothed wheel of cast iron, on the upper

surface of which, continuous with the surface of the
box itself, is placed a circuit of ellipsoidal friction
rollers, kept in their places by a flanch on a moveable
ring of iron, and playing between the upper surface
of the box and the under surface of the top plate of
the frame. By the arrangements thus far described,
it will be perceived that the screw may rise and fall
by revolving on its own axis, carrying with it the
platten attached to its lower extremity by means of
a knob or head of well known application. The
screw is made to revolve, by four arms fastened to
the body thereof, just above the platten. With this
arrangement the machine, in point of action, differs
in no respect from the common screw-press, but may
be quickly turned in either direction, involving no
serious loss of time in bringing the platten to and
from its work. When, however, the pressure becomes too intense to allow the workman longer to
turn the screw, the arms just mentioned are made
stationary by a plug or plugs set into the platten,
and the box itself is turned by means of a horizontal
tangent screw applied to the tangent wheel already
described. It is now that the friction rollers come
into play, preventing, to a considerable extent, the
resistance which would otherwise proceed from the
action of the box against the roller in the top block
against which it plays. The axis of the screw has
a winch of convenient length, by which it may be
turned as long as it is thought practicable ; and it
also carries a toothed wheel, which is capable of

being acted on by a pinion of much smaller diameter,
that may be thrown into gear at pleasure, and to
which the winch may be then transferred.   This
third and last mode of giving motion to the press is
only required when extreme pressure is to be communicated.

"The Committee think the advantage of three rates
of speed in this press will commend it to the attention of manufacturers, who have often found cause
to complain of the loss of time involved by the common hydrostatic-press, with a single forcing-pump,
and equally so by those screw presses in which the
whole range of motion was to be effected by a com-
paratively slow process.

"As the inventor does not confine himself to any
particular scale of dimensions, we have not deemed
it necessary to make a statement of the calculation
applicable to the press which we have examined,
further than to remark, that it multiplies the force
applied 10,000 times, and when operated on by a
single man capable of applying sixty-six pounds,
may, exclusive of friction, apply a pressure amount-
ing to about 200 tons.

"WILLIAM HAMILTON, Actuary.
"June 11, 1835."

THE ARMING PRESS.

The next important press is that used for giving
to the covers of books many of those decorations
which could not be done by hand or through the me-

dium of the presses above described, from the inadequate pressure of the one, and the liability of error in the other.   Arming presses are manufactured of various sizes, and according to the taste of different makers, varying in design.   The principle of all is nearly the same, and we shall therefore, to avoid repetition, confine the description to the *Imperial Arming Press*, invented by Messrs. Cope and Sherwin, of Cumberland Street, Curtain Road, Shoreditch, London, which is on the same principle as their Imperial Printing Press.   The Frontispiece, plate VII., will display the general outline of the staple or standard of the press.   The bed plate is constructed with a contrivance for raising or lowering it, according to the thickness of the plate to be applied.   This is effected by means of two series of circular inclined planes, placed one above the other, similar to the clutch box used for engaging and disengaging certain parts of machinery.   When placed in the proper position, it is fastened by a pall which takes into a ratchet on its lower edge.   Upon the bed are fixed two parallel rulers at right angles to each other, to insure precision in the work.   The carriage on which the bed is placed, traverses backward and forward by means of a screw put in motion by the handle in front.   On the piston which supports the heater box, to which the plate or die is to be fixed, is seen the adjusting screw ; and under the projecting head of the press a strong spring is attached, to raise and support the piston, with the heaters, &c.   In front of the heater box, or platten, are holes for the two heating-irons, and between them the groove in which the design is fixed. The impression is given by means of the handle, which working on the connecting rods at the top, causes the main bolt or axis, which in a state of rest lies in an angular position, to assume a perpendicular one, thereby driving down the piston with great force; exerting a pressure adequate to the power and system of levers upon which it has been employed.

Others are manufactured by the same gentlemen, having two cheeks instead of one main supporter, and for small designs, where time is saved by not moving the carriage, but laying on the book, guided by the square, and taking the impression, are preferable. But for working off large toolings and embossments, or extensive letterings, this press is invaluable to the bookbinder. To many other purposes all of them may be applied with equal advantage. The largest description of embossed covers, &c. are executed by means of a fly press of enormous power.

THE CUTTING PRESS.

The cutting or laying press is formed of two strong cheeks of timber, connected together with two wooden screws and two square pins. These screws are from two to three feet in length; the heads, in which are two large holes to introduce the pin, by which the books are firmly pinched between the cheeks, project out on the right side as seen in figure

2. of plate V. The screws are held firmly in the
right cheek by two bolts, and in the left are cut
worms for the screws to work in. On one side of
the left cheek are fixed two slips of wood an inch and
a half asunder, which forms a groove for the cheek
of the plough to run in. This side of the press is
used for cutting only. The other, which presents an
even surface on each cheek, is applied to every other
purpose where the laying press is required.

HARDIE'S CUTTING PRESS.

This press, an invention of Mr. James Hardie,
bookbinder of Glasgow, obtained a considerable share
of attention from the trade in Glasgow and Edinburgh when first produced (A.D. 1805.) The Society
of Arts of London also voted the inventor the sum of
fifteen guineas. The principal difference between it
and the one described consists in being worked with
one iron screw in place of two wooden ones. Instead
of two cheeks, it presents a square frame, having
a moving piece or cheek, which slides in grooves
within the two sides of the frame; the screw works
in a nut let into the right-hand side of the frame,
its lower end working in a collar, screwed to the
moving piece. Though, at first, it was said to be
more simple and powerful than the common press,
and adapted to work more economically, it has not
by any means been generally adopted. This press
is accurately represented in the engraving, figure 2,
plate VIII.

THE PLOUGH.

This is so connected with the cutting press, that it would not be proper to speak of it in any other than the present place. It consists of two light cheeks, drawn together by a single screw in the centre, and regulated by two pins, one on each side. In the right cheek is cut a groove, the thickness of the knife, which is fixed to it by means of an iron bolt, passing through the cheek, having a screw at the top to allow of its being firmly secured by a nut. The other cheek fits in the groove on the cutting press. See plate V., figure 2.

THE FINISHING PRESS

Is exactly similar in construction to the LAYING PRESS, but smaller, and without any groove for the plough; further description, therefore, will not be necessary.

THE SEWING PRESS,

Represented in figure 1, plate V., is formed of a bed of hard wood, having an opening extending within a few inches of each end, and an inch from the front edge. At each end of the bed is fixed a wooden screw, furnished with nuts to support the cross bar, on which the strings are fastened. This bar rises or falls, as the nuts are raised or lowered.

THE ROLLING MACHINE,

Intended to supersede the necessity of beating, is

P

a late invention. It is accurately figured in the annexed engraving, No. I., and we refer the reader to
page 15, for a description of the manner in which
the work is passed through it. The power of compression is given by the two iron cylinders, which are
about a foot in diameter, the upper one of which can
be regulated by means of the handle seen at the
head, to any pressure required. On the frame, in a
line with the space between the rollers, is placed a
table or board, for beating the book up even, and
more steadily passing it through. The handle of the
wheel in front, being turned by a powerful man,
gives motion to the others, and thus exerts a force
on the rollers in a proportion of five-sixths over that
of beating. A committee of the Society of Arts in-
spected one of these machines, and gave a highly
favourable report of it. Among other works that
was pressed before them, was a minion Bible, which
was passed through the press in one minute. Mr.
Burn was presented with the Society's silver Vulcan
medal for his invention. For offices where much
work is done, this press must be invaluable, from the
great saving of time required in beating; but it may
be doubtful if ever they can be applied with advantage generally throughout the country.

THE RULING MACHINE.

Figure 3, in the engraving VIII., shows the principle of the *ruling machine*. It is simple in construction, but remarkable for the facility and precision

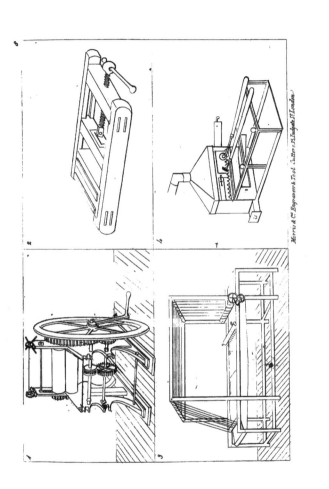

Morris & C? Engravers & Tool Cutters 35 Ludgate St London.

with which the most complicated and difficult patterns are executed by it. The general framework, it will be seen, is plain, and requires no description. The bed is made of baize, the ends sewn well together, and the exterior surface painted over to make it firm and smooth. This is placed round rollers at each end, which being turned by means of the winch, carries the paper laid on, under the pens, and passes round below the machine. The cords seen passing over the head, confine the paper firmly on the bed. These revolve on four rollers, one at each angle, having grooves for the cords, and are also set in motion by the winch. The pens for making the lines are let into the slide in the centre, and firmly fixed by screws underneath. The slide can be momentarily lifted up by the catch on the side, where head lines or blank spaces are required. The ink is placed in pieces of double-milled flannel attached to the slide at the head of the pens, which being kept well supplied, the ink flows gradually and equally down as required. Where inks of different colours, such as red and blue, are necessary in one pattern, another slide is fixed at a short distance from the other, and both ruled at the same time. The near side of the machine, being at right angles with the slide, the paper, which is cut true before ruling, is kept perfectly square by it.

Ruling pens are made of thin brass, cut up about an inch of their length, and formed by bending the two sides together, and cutting the ends to an exact point, leaving sufficient space for the ink to flow down the centre.

THE STATIONER'S CUTTING PRESS.

This press is similar to the one before described, but rests at each end on pivots, by which means the screws hang downwards, and the cheeks of the press are brought in a line with a table on the side. On this table a square is fixed, by which means the paper is placed in the press quicker, and a certainty insured of its being cut true.

Another mode adopted by some stationers requires description, being the readiest and most true of any other. A hand-screw is attached to a beam above, and hangs perpendicularly. Under this is placed a block, on which is fixed what may be termed the cutting-board, or table. The paper being laid open and even upon it, a board perfectly square and to the size of the paper is placed in the centre, and the screw above brought upon it and firmly tightened. This board has a groove for the plough, of a peculiar construction, to work in on every side. The plough being placed in one of the grooves, is then gradually worked in a similar way to the *carpenter's* plough, with both hands, till the whole of the paper is cut through : the other three sides are then in like manner cut, the screw unloosed, and the paper, which will be the exact size of the board, and perfectly square, taken away.

THE STATIONER'S PLOUGH.

The plough used for the common press is also the same as before spoken of, but the one used in the process last named will require description. It is formed of two cheeks, in the centre of the right-hand side one of which the knife is fixed by a bolt. This is similar in shape to the common knife, but fastened in a groove in a perpendicular position, the point being even with the edge, which is of iron. The other cheek, which works in the groove on the board, is let into the first, and rises gradually as the knife descends in cutting through the paper.

PENNY'S CUTTING PRESS.

The above are convenient and efficient machines in the hands of experienced workmen, but it requires much practice to obtain any thing like precision in their use. Various attempts have been made to produce a press possessing the means of adjusting itself, and insuring perfect accuracy, independent of any degree of skill possessed by the workman. Mr. Penny's attention had long been drawn to these facts, and he has succeeded in producing a machine possessing many novelties and improvements. This has been attained by introducing a moveable stage for receiving the paper or book to be cut, which being always parallel with the surface of the press, insures the requisite precision in cutting, all the edges being parallel to, or at right angles with each other.

The press consists of two cheeks like the common one. The two screws are of iron, and the moveable bed is raised or lowered by turning them. The two screws are turned by means of four cog-wheels, beneath the bottom of the press, motion being given, through the medium of a handle on the upright shaft of the wheel, to the centre ·wheel, which turns the others carrying the screws.

This press offers many great advantages : besides insuring perfect accuracy of workmanship, twice the usual quantity of paper, may be cut at once, and with greater rapidity. In cutting and gilding of highly-glazed and other paper, there is no danger of falling through.

From the quantity and quality of workmanship necessarily expended in constructing one of these presses, they are much more expensive than the common press. About 30*l.*

PENNY'S PLOUGH.

To effect the greatest possible accuracy in cutting, the above gentleman has also invented a plough suitable to the press. The knife is fixed with two bolts, and the blade placed exactly under the screw. The bed for the knife is of metal, and the knife accurately finished, so that no tedious adjustment is ever necessary. Mr. Penny received a reward for this invention from the Society of Arts.

WATTS' PAMPHLET PIERCER.

Printed sheets stitched into pamphlets, and other small works, are pierced through the edge of the uncut side with three holes, and are united by a single thread, passed through the hole and tied in a knot. The instrument used for piercing the sheets, is a common awl, assisted when necessary by a mallet; and as this work is done by women, it often becomes a laborious and even painful operation.

Mr. Philip Watts was applied to by a woman occupied in pamphlet stitching, to invent a machine which should diminish the labour and expedite the work, and the result was the instrument about to be described. The bottom is a strong board, on which are raised ledges on the top and side, placed at right angles, so as to form two sides of a square. The side is fixed in its position by means of screws; the head is moveable for a few inches, to enable a pamphlet of any usual size to be laid against the side bar, having the middle of its back directly under the three needles. The adjustable ledge has a plate screwed to its under side, which slides into the bottom board, and is fastened to its position by a nut. On the outside of the side ledge, a standard is firmly fixed to the board by a screw nut underneath, having two short pieces projecting, and a square groove at their ends; on each of which is applied, by means of two binding-screws, another square groove, thus forming two rectangular holes, or guides for the bar. On the top of the bar is a connecting-rod, joining the bar with the lever, the fulcrum of which is a pin at the top of the standard. At the bottom of the bar is a transverse piece, with three tapering grooves, which receive and hold steadily the upper ends of the tapering needles, these latter being still farther secured by a face-plate.

The method of using this machine is self-evident. The sheets being laid evenly one on another, and adjusted by means of the ledges, the handle of the lever is brought down. The effect of this action is to depress the bar, and to force the needles through the sheets. The motion of the needles being vertical, there is little likelihood of their being broken; but if this should happen, it is only necessary to take off the face-plate, to remove the broken needle, and to substitute a perfect one in its place.

Mr. Watts was presented with five pounds by the Society of Arts for his invention.

TOOLS, &c. USED IN FORWARDING.

No particular arrangement can be made of the articles requisite for executing the various processes in binding: we shall therefore describe them as nearly as possible in the rotation in which they are used. The first, therefore, will be

THE FOLDER,

which is a long flat piece of bone or ivory with two edges, and rounded at each extremity; used in folding the sheets of a work, and many other manipulations.

THE BEATING HAMMER.

This is shown in the engraving, fig. 3, plate V., and is varied in shape according to the taste of the maker, and weighs from ten to fourteen pounds. The face is well rounded off.

THE BEATING STONE.

A solid polished body, generally of black marble, and fixed upon a firm block of wood. The stone, and manner of beating, is shown in the plate last referred to.

THE SAW.

For forming the fissures for the cords on which a book is sewn, is what is called a tenant saw, and too well known to need description.

THE KEYS.

Used for attaching the strings in sewing firmly to the foot of the sewing press. They are made of brass, and their form various, though the one seen on the engraved sketch of the sewing-press is considered the best.

THE PARING KNIFE,

Is what cutlers call a sword blade, being pointed at the end, and long, so as to admit of its paring the leather very thin.

THE PLOUGH-KNIFE,

Which is fixed to the plough by a bolt and screw

as before described, is about six inches long and
finely pointed, the point being the part that cuts the
book, &c., as the plough is moved backward and
forward. The new patent plough-knife is considered very superior.

THE COMPASSES

Are large and small, the latter having a spring,
and used by the gilder ; the former strong in the joint,
so as not to be easily moved when set to the size of
the book, &c., to insure correctness in marking many
volumes to the same size.

THE BODKIN.

A strong point of iron fixed in wood, to form the
holes in the boards required to lace in the bands :
used also in marking the lines for cutting, &c.

THE SHEARS,

Large and small, the latter requiring no description. The large are formed of two long pieces of
iron ; one of which being fixed in the end of the laying press, the power of the hand on the other will
cause it to easily cut through milled boards, &c.,
required for the side covers. These shears are about
four feet long.

THE SQUARE.

Two pieces of wood or iron firmly fixed at right
angles to each other, one having a falling grove to

fix to the side of the board, so as to cause the other to be truly marked on it.

THE BACKING HAMMER.

A flat round-headed hammer, similar to those used by shoemakers. It is employed in backing the book, and every other process where the hammer is required.

KNOCKING DOWN IRON.

A flat piece of iron with a centre-piece placed at right angles, to fix in the end of the laying press. Used for beating down the strings after lacing in the side-boards.

THE GRATER, OR RAKE.

An instrument armed with dents or teeth, which serves to scrape the back of the books when in the press, after boarding, to make the back hard and firm.

THE SCRAPER.

This is used by the gilder of edges to scrape the surface perfectly smooth. It is usually made of a piece of clock-spring, or blade of an elastic steel knife.

THE BURNISHER.

Is an agate, fixed in a long staff of wood, and used to burnish the edges of books. Sometimes a pair of dog's teeth, which bend somewhat to the shape, are used.

THE WATER TUB.

An indispensable article, which anything water tight will answer the purpose of.

BOARDS.

Boards used in bookbinding are of various kinds, viz.

Pressing Boards, which are generally made of beech, and according to the size, of different thicknesses, all being perfectly even and smooth throughout the whole extent.

Backing Boards.—Thin pieces of wood of various lengths, thicker on the top than the bottom, and bevelled off so as to present a sharp edge to the side of the book where the grooves for the boards are to be formed. The edges are sometimes cased with iron.

Cutting Boards.—Similar to the above, but having a smooth square top to direct the knife true, and to insure the book being put even in the press.

Burnishing Boards.—In shape nearly like the above, varying only in those being thicker at one end than the other that are employed for the head or tail of the book.

THE MARBLING TROUGH

Is generally made of oak, all the joints being well put together to make it water-tight. The most useful is about thirty inches long, eighteen or twenty wide, and two or three inches deep. For the economy of size, &c., where a few books are required to be marbled, the trough may be divided into compartments, by ribs formed to fit in or remove at pleasure.

THE WINCH.

This is a cylinder of wood, mounted on an axle of iron, and used for pulling down the standing press, as shown in the engraving, plate V., figure 4.

THE SHAVING TUB,

Over which is placed the cutting press, as seen in the engraving, is a frame of wood for holding the shavings, &c., from the cutting of the edges. It is so called from it being usual in early times to place the press across a tub.

BRUSHES

Of various sizes, and such as are used by painters, with

VASES OR POTS

Of varnished earthenware or delf, will be found requisite in many of the stages of binding. These complete the articles required in forwarding.

TOOLS, &c., REQUIRED BY THE FINISHER.

The same arrangement as for the tools of the forwarder must here also be adopted.

THE GOLD KNIFE.

This knife, used for cutting the gold, is eight or ten inches long, with a short handle, the blade being highly tempered, and sharpened on both sides similar to a painter's pallet knife.

Q

THE GOLD CUSHION,

Formed of an oblong piece of board, covered with calf, the flesh side upwards, under which is placed several layers of flannel, or uniformly stuffed with wool.

THE TRINDLE,

Is simply a piece of thin lath with which the gilder passes the gold from the cushion to the edges of the book when gilding.

THE TIP.

Used in a similar manner by the gilder in covering the back and sides with gold.   It is made of card board, having sable between the two pieces of which it is formed.

LETTERS OR ALPHABETS.

Are of all sizes, cut in brass, and fixed in wooden handles, about six inches in length.   There are also alphabets of

BRASS TYPE,

Cut short and made to fit in a *hand chase*, whereby the entire lettering of a volume can be adjusted to the proper breadth, and fixed on the volume at one time, instead of by single letters.   Where a great number of volumes of the same work are binding, this effects a very considerable saving of time.

TOOLS.

This name is given to such ornaments as are cut

9

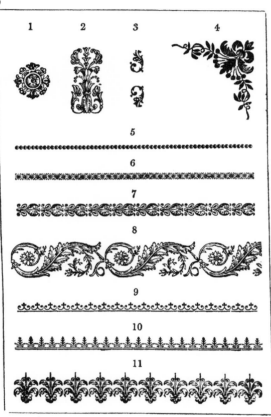

in brass and fixed in handles like letters. These are
generally applied on the backs or books, and are of
various descriptions, as seen in plate IX. They are
known by several technical names; viz. number 1, a
star; 2, a flower or sprig; 3, scrolls; and 4, a corner.

PALLETS

Are also of brass, three or four inches long, and
ornamented throughout. They are fixed in handles
like tools, generally the patterns of rolls, and used
for gilding the bands of books.

ROLLS.

A kind of brass wheel, on the face of which is cut
the figure intended to be impressed; they are of various patterns, from a single line, which is called a
fillet, up to the most elaborate and classical designs.
They are mounted on an iron carriage, made to receive the axle of the roll, which is firmly fixed in a
long wooden handle, that rests against the shoulder
when used. The second figure lying on the stove,
plate VIII., shows the shape of the roll. The annexed plate displays some of the diversified patterns
of this ornament. They are thus technically denominated, No. 5, bead roll; 6, 7, 8, running borders; and 9, 10, 11, vandyke patterns.

BLOCKS.

Lettering pieces with ornamental borders cut in
solid brass, and executed with the arming-press, are

called blocks. These are worked on the sides or backs of books, according to fancy. The great expense of providing blocks for such work has long been matter of regret, and confined the use of this sort of ornament. This has led to a consideration of the subject, and to the construction of an ingenious and simple instrument, by Morris and Co., which they call the

TYPOGRAPHICAL ACCELERATOR,

And which is well adapted for ornamental side and back lettering pieces. These will entirely supersede the use of blocks, and enable the binder to proceed with his work without the delay heretofore occasioned. The design is formed with a number of separate ornaments fitting exactly into each other : thus, when the number of any design is worked off, it can be taken to pieces, and any other, from the size of a folio to a 32mo. executed. For the better working of these designs, the same parties have also produced a small

LETTERING PRESS,

represented in the opposite engraving. The block or lettering, which is kept warm by a heater, is fixed in the slide at the bottom of the piston, and brought down by the motion of the projecting arms at the top. It is simple and expeditious, and the cost trifling.

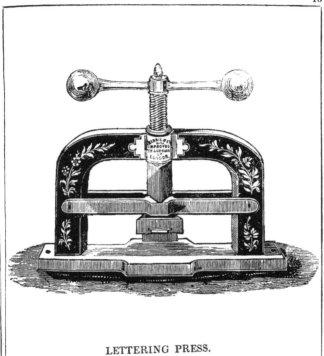

LETTERING PRESS.

ARMORIAL BEARINGS.

These are solid plates of brass, on which are cut the arms of such families who may wish to have their books ornamented with their heraldic insignia. Under this head, too, might be considered

ARABESQUE PLATES.

Which are also in solid brass, and imprinted on the leather by means of the arming press.

BILLETS.

Square or inclined blocks of wood used for placing the book on, or between, during the operation of gilding.

THE POLISHER

Is a bar of iron an inch in diameter, and a foot long, bent a little forward at bottom. At the end a transverse bar of iron, about three inches round and four long, is fixed, having a highly polished surface on the circular part intended to act on the book. The shape is shown in the near figure on the stove. This iron is fixed in a wooden handle like the rolls. Another polisher for the back and bands is used; instead of being round at bottom, it is brought out to nearly a fine edge so as to admit of its polishing close to the bands on the back.

THE STOVE.

The stove of the Finisher varies much. In large

q 3

offices in London, an open pan, with niches for each letter round the edge, is most generally used. In smaller they differ, are of varied shapes, some being open, and some having small apertures round the sides. Considering the general utility, we give an engraving of one which we deem will be found to answer every purpose of the gilder, being the most commodious and most perfect we know, and one which can be made, from the description we shall give, in any place, at a small expense. See figure 4, plate VIII.

The framework consists of the stove, the cap which receives the smoke, &c., which escapes from the charcoal, and the pipe or tunnel which conducts it above. Within is placed a grill of iron, on which the charcoal rests. Under this is a large opening for the introduction of air necessary for combustion. This opening may be shut by the door seen traversing the bars of the part in front. On this side is a drawer, which serves to receive the ashes of the charcoal. Above the fire-place are two large openings, which may be entirely closed, or the contrary, by a door on each side (which move on vertical hinges), according as the heat is wished to be increased or diminished. One of these doors is shown open. All this part of the stove is constructed of thin plate iron. The base of the part in front is also of plate iron, and all the rest constructed of small iron rods, as shown in the engraving.

GRAINING PLATES.

These are cut in copper and brass, and are the size of the forms of different books. For the cross-grain, fine wire is tightly crossed from side to side, at regular distances, and the whole run over evenly with solder.

It may be further remarked, that the finisher will also require a gold-rag, some fine cotton-wool, camels'-hair pencils, sponges, and brushes, but these will need no description.

We have now treated of every thing connected with this part of our subject, and brought to a close our endeavours to lay before the Trade minute particulars of every manipulation in the various branches of the Art of Bookbinding, as well as a description of the Tools required for their proper execution. It remains only to add such matters as could not be introduced therein, and which will be found in the following Appendix.

APPENDIX.

―――――

ON BLEACHING, &c.

IT is necessary that the binder should be conversant with the best methods for taking out any stains that may, from accident, have been communicated to paper, and also for giving to it a better colour. We shall, therefore, lay down the most simple but approved methods for rendering the material as clear as possible.

There are two ways of whitening paper, viz. by submitting it to the action of vapour, and to that of acids diluted in water. We shall place these, as well as the other receipts, under their proper heads, describing the manipulations peculiar to each method.

ON BLEACHING PAPER GROWN YELLOW BY AGE, &c.

The best proceeding known is the one given by M. Chaptal, and long used by the trade. It is commenced by cutting the bands and separating the sheets, which should be placed in cases formed in a leaden tub, with very thin slips of wood, so that the sheets rest on a plate separated one from the other by intervals scarcely sensible; then pour into the tub *oxymuriatic acid* or *chlorine*, taking care that it falls upon the sides so that the leaves are not deranged by the motion. When the workman judges by the whiteness of the paper that it has been sufficiently acted upon, the acid is drawn off by a little cock placed at the bottom of the tub, and its place supplied with fresh clear water several times, to take off, and deprive it of the smell of the acid. The leaves are placed to dry, afterwards pressed, and then re-bound.

The leaves might be placed vertically in the tub, which position presents some advantages, from the sheets not being so liable to tear. M. Chaptal constructed a frame of wood, adjusted to the size of the paper. This frame contained very thin slips of wood, with intervals between them. In each of these intervals two leaves were placed, held to their positions by small wooden wedges forced between them, so as to press them against the sides of the slips. This proceeding is more preferable from the frame being easily raised and plunged into fresh water.

By these means not only are the leaves cleaned, but the paper receives a degree of whiteness it never before possessed. The acid also removes stains of ink, which are often found to disfigure a book.

Another plan is to steep the leaves in a caustic solution of soda prepared as follows :—With a certain weight of the *subcarbonate of soda* or *potash*, mix half the quantity of *quicklime*; then add soft water, and boil. The liquor, when cold, is the solution of *caustic alkali*. As the causticity of the alkalies depends on their freedom from carbonic acid,

which the quick-lime absorbs, it is necessary that the
solution should be kept from exposure to the atmos-
phere, which restores to it the carbonic acid, and
thereby destroys its caustic properties. When perfectly bleached, arrange the sheets on lines to dry, or
place them between cloths, in the same manner as
paper-makers dispose their sheets of paper when
delivered from the form. When quite dry, press
them between glazed boards, and the texture of the
paper will be the same as at first.

A solution of *chlorine of lime* has been found to
have a good effect, restoring in a few minutes engravings, &c., very much stained with smoke and
damp.

Some consider submitting the paper to the action
of vapour preferable to steeping, as above directed.
Sulphuric acid gas removes very readily the yellow
colour which age gives to paper. The use of this
will require some precaution; and to operate more
effectually, it is proper to be provided with a large
chest, perfectly air tight, so as to prevent the escape
of the gas. In this chest, a number of small cords
must be disposed, very near each other, and on which
the paper is placed. On each side is formed an opening, which is glazed, and well fastened round, so that
the progress of the operation may be observed, and
the paper withdrawn the instant it is sufficiently
bleached. The ignition of the sulphur should not be
made in the chest, as a risk is hazarded of blacking
the paper, but in a little furnace placed on the side

without, and the sulphuric vapour directed by a pipe into it. The sulphur is then put by degrees upon an iron plate placed over the fire, so as to keep up a supply of vapour till the operation is completed.

The same precautions will be necessary in using *chlorine*, or *oxymuriatic acid*, in a state of gas. After disposing the paper on the cords, place in a cup a spoonful of *muriatic acid*, (spirits of salts), and put round it another of *oxyde of manganese* (red lead); then place this cup in a vessel filled with hot water, and place it on the fire; it thus gives out a large portion of gas, by which the chamber is filled, as before directed.

ON TAKING OUT STAINS OF INK, OIL, AND GREASE.

Oxymuriatic acid, or *chlorine*, removes perfectly stains of ink; and should the paper require bleaching, the operation will answer both ends at the same time; but as it more frequently happens that the stains are the only blemish necessary to remove, the proceedings are given for taking them out without pulling to pieces the volume.

Nearly all the acids remove spots of ink from paper, but it is important to use such as attack its texture the least. *Spirits of salts*, diluted in five or six times the quantity of water, may be applied with success upon the spot, and after a minute or two washing it off with clear water. A solution of *oxalic acid, citric acid*, or *tartaric acid* is attended with the least risk, and may be applied upon the paper and plates without fear of damage. These acids taking out writing ink, and not touching the printing, can be used for restoring books where the margins have been written upon, without attacking the text.

When the paper is disfigured with stains of iron, it may be perfectly restored by applying a solution of *sulphuret of potash*, and afterwards one of *oxalic acid*. The sulphuret extracts from the iron part of its oxygen, and renders it soluble in the diluted acids.

A simple, but at the same time a very effectual method of raising spots of grease, wax, oil, or any other fat substance, is by washing the part with *ether*, and by placing it between white blotting paper. Then with a hot iron press above the parts stained, and the defect will be speedily removed. In many cases, where the stains are not bad, rectified *spirits of wine* will be found to answer the purpose.

The most expeditious, and by some binders considered the best, mode of removing grease from paper is, to scrape fine pipe clay on both sides of the stain, and apply a hot iron above, taking especial care that it is not too hot, whereby the paper might be scorched. The same process will remove grease from coloured calf, and if the spot should even be on the under side of the leather it may be thus cleanly drawn through. For dirty-fingered workmen this must be invaluable.

Imison, in his Elements of Science, gives the following receipt for taking out spots of grease, and which has been very generally adopted. " After having gently warmed the paper that is stained with grease, take out as much as possible by means of blotting paper, then dip a small brush in the essential oil of turpentine, heated almost to ebullition, and draw it gently over both sides of the paper, which must be carefully kept warm. This operation must be repeated as many times as the quantity of the fat imbibed by the paper, or the thickness of the paper may render necessary. When the greasy substance is entirely removed, recourse may be had to the following method to restore the paper to its former whiteness, which is not completely restored by the first process. Dip another brush in highly rectified spirit of wine, and draw it in like manner over the place which was stained, and particularly round the edges, to remove the border that would still present a stain. By employing these means with proper caution, the spot will totally disappear, the paper will resume its original whiteness, and if the process have been employed on a part written with common ink, or printed with printer's ink, it will experience no alteration."

ON GIVING CONSISTENCE TO BAD PAPER.

The method used in Germany was first communicated from Strasburg by M. de Regemorte, who had made many researches on the subject, and will be found the best. This plan not only gives to paper an additional firmness, but a better colour. It consists of making a strong size, in a proportion of one ounce of isinglass, dissolved in a quart of water, and boiled

over the fire, to which afterwards add a quarter of a
pound of alum, and when dissolved, filter through a
sieve. The paper must be passed through the size,
at a heat wherein the hand may be held, then placed
on lines to dry gradually, not exposed to the sun in
summer, or a room too warm in winter, and afterwards pressed.

HOT AND COLD PRESSING.

The presser should be provided with a considerable
number of glazed boards, &c. This art, which
appears very simple, requires a good knowledge of the
qualities of different papers, each of these qualities
demanding the precautions which it is impossible to
describe, and for which general rules only could be
given. A little practice will render this soon easy.
The proceedings are so well known, that they need no
description.

ON THE SCENT OF RUSSIA.

The peculiar scent of russia leather, so esteemed as
a cover for books, is given with the *empyreumatic oil
of the birch.* The bark of this tree is also used in
northern Europe in tanning. Many researches have
been made by distinguished chymists, but at present
no method that can be decided effectual in its results
has been made known. It remains, however, for the
scientific to consider how far the oil above-mentioned
may be employed to cause other leather to give out
the peculiar odour of russia.

ON PERFUMING BOOKS.

Musk, with one or two drops of *oil of neroli*, sponged on each side of the leaves and hung up to dry, will give them a powerful odour. A more simple proceeding is to put a phial containing this mixture into the bookcase, or place on various parts of the shelves pieces of cotton wool, well impregnated with *oil of birch* or *cedar*.

ON DESTROYING WORMS.

There is a small insect, *Aglossa pinguinalis*, that deposits its larvæ in books in the autumn, especially in the leaves nearest the cover. These gradually produce a kind of mites, doing the binding no little injury. But the little wood-boring beetles, *anobium pertinax* and *striatum*, are the most destructive. M. Peignot mentions an instance where, in a public library but little frequented, *twenty-seven* folio volumes were perforated in a straight line by the same insect, in such a manner that, on passing a cord through the perfectly round hole made by it, these twenty-seven volumes could be raised at once. The seat of the mischief appears to lie in the binding, and the best preventive against their attacks is mineral salts, to which all insects have an aversion. *Alum* and *vitriol* are proper for this purpose, and it would be advisable to mix a portion with the paste used for covering the books. M. Prediger, among other instructions to German bookbinders, advises them to

make their paste of starch instead of flour.   He also
recommends them to slightly powder the books, the
covers, and even the shelves on which they stand,
with a mixture of powdered alum and fine pepper;
and is of opinion that in the months of March, July,
and September, books should be rubbed with a piece
of woollen cloth, steeped in a solution of powdered
alum, and dried.

SHELL GOLD.

Grind up gold leaf with honey, in a mortar ; then
wash away the honey with water, and mix the gold
powder with gum-water. This may be applied to
any substance with a camel's hair pencil, in the same
way as any other colour.

PASTE.

Flour paste for cementing is formed principally of
wheaten flour boiled in water till it becomes of a glu-
tinous or viscid consistence.   It may be prepared of
these ingredients simply for common purposes, but
the paste proper for bookbinding should have mixed
with the flour a sixth or eighth part of its weight of
powdered alum, and if it is wanted still more tena-
cious, gum arabic, or any kind of size, may be added.

TECHNICAL TERMS

ART OF BOOKBINDING

Arms.—Plates on which are engraved, in relief, armorial bearings, usually gilt on the sides of books belonging to the libraries of the nobility.

Asterisk.—A sign used by the printers at the bottom of the front page of the duplicate leaves printed to supply the place of those cancelled.

Bands.—The strings whereon the sheets of a volume are sewn, which are either let in by sewing the back, or project from the back. This term also applies to pieces of leather glued on the back previous to covering the book, and used merely for ornament. The space between two of these is called *between bands.*

Bands.—Name given to bindings simply covered with leather in the tanned state. Thus we say, *in sheep bands.*

Basil.—Sheep skin tanned, used for common bindings.

Bead.—The little knot of the headband.

Beating.—A section of sheets of a work taken at one time, and beat with the hammer upon the stone.

Bleed.—A work is said to bleed, if cut into the print.

Blind-Tooled.—Where the book is ornamented with the gilding-tools, but without gold.

Boards.—The name given to the pieces of wood used in the various processes of pressing, backing, cutting, and burnishing of the work ; also, the side covers of the book.

Boards, in.—When the edges of a book are cut after the boards have been laced in. *Out of boards*, when cut first. Where the book is covered with paper or cloth, it is also called *in boards.*

Bosses.—The plates of brass attached to the sides of large volumes, for their greater preservation.

Cancels.—Leaves containing errors, which are to be cut out and replaced with others printed correctly ; and generally given with the last sheet of a book.

Case Work.—Where the covers are prepared before placing on the volume.

Catch-Word.—A word met with in early printed books at the bottom of the last page of each sheet, which word is the first of the page which follows in the next.

Chain-Stitch.—The stitch which the sewer makes at the head and tail of the volume previous to commencing another course.

Collating.—This operation is common to the gatherer, folder, and binder. It is the examining of the sheets, to see that the signatures properlv follow, to prevent any transposition whereby the work would be rendered imperfect.

Corners.—The triangular brass tools used as ornaments on the corners of the sides of books. The pieces of brass fixed on stationery bindings ; also the pieces of leather pasted on the corners of half-bound books.

Cropping.—The cutting down of a book near the print.

Double Book.—When a book is printed in half sheets, it is called a double book.

Drawing in.—The operation of fastening the boards to the back of the volume, with the bands on which it is sewn.

End Papers.—The blank leaves placed at the beginning and end of a volume.

Extra ; as Calf-extra.—Is a term applied to the style of binding, when the book is well forwarded, lined with good marble paper. has silk headbands, and gilt with a narrow roll round the sides and inside the squares.

Finisher.—The workman who executes the colouring, gilding, and other ornamental operations of binding.

Filleted.—Is when the bands of a volume are marked with a single gilt line only.

Folder.—The party who folds the book according to the pages, previous to its being bound or boarded. This department in large towns is generally done by females.

Fore-edge.—The front edge of the book.

Forwarder.—The workman who performs all the operations of binding, up to the colouring.

Foot-line.—The line at the bottom of the first page of each sheet, under which is placed the signature.

Gatherer.—The name given to the workman who classes the printed sheets of a volume according to the signatures.

Gathering.—A portion of ten or twelve sheets of a volume, as made up previous to folding; thus, a work is said to consist of two, three, or more gatherings.

Gilder.—In London and great towns, the workman who gilds the edges of books; also applied to the one who gilds the backs and sides.

Gilt.—A book bound firm and strong, having plain end-papers and gilt back.

Glaire.—Name given to the whites of eggs used in the process of gilding.

Grooves.—The projections formed on the sides of the books in backing, to admit of the boards laying even with the back when laced in.

Guards.—Shreds of strong paper interspersed and sewn to the backs of books, intended for the insertion of prints, &c., to prevent the book being uneven when filled. Also the pieces projecting over the end-papers.

Gutter.—The round front edge of a volume, formed by flattening the circular back previous to cutting.

Half-bound—When the back and corners of a book only are covered with leather, and the sides with coloured or marble paper.

Half-extra—Books forwarded carefully, and lined with common marble paper, having silk headbands, and narrow rolled round the sides with gold, but plain inside.

Head.—The top of the volume.

Headband.—The silk or cotton ornament worked at the top and bottom of the back.

Headline.—The line immediately under the running-title on the pages of a book.

Inset—The pages cut off in folding, and placed in the middle of the folded sheet.

Justification.—The observance that the pages of works, bound in one volume, agree in length and breadth, so as to insure their not being cut into the print.

Kettle-stitch.—A corruption of chain-stitch.

Lettered.—Volumes simply filleted on the back, and the title lettered.

Lines.—A book is said to be in *morocco lines*, when the only ornament is a plain fillet on the bands and round the sides.

Lining the Boards.—Pasting paper on the boards before fixing them to the volume, to give them more firmness.

Marbler.—The workman who marbles the edges of books, &c.

Nose.—In glueing up a volume, if the workman has not been careful to make all the sheets occupy a right line at the head, it will present a point either at the beginning or end, which point is called *a nose.*

Overcasting.—An operation in sewing, where the work consists of single leaves or plates, the thread being brought over the back and the needle pierced through the paper near the band.

Pallet.—Name given to the tools used in gilding the bands.
Paring.—Bringing down with the knife the edges of leather, &c., to avoid the projections they would otherwise make.
Patch.—The piece of leather, placed over the defects sometimes found in common substances.
Points.—Terms of gathering and folding. They are two holes made in the sheets in the process of printing, to insure, in turning, what is called good register. These holes serve as a guide in certain folds which are made by the folder.

Quire.—The same as a gathering.

Register, or *Registrum Chartarum.*—A list of signatures and first words of sheets, attached to the end of early printed works for the use of the binder, but now long disused.
Registers.—Ribbons fastened under the headband, left hanging at the foot, to denote the place where the reader may have left off.
Rolls.—The cylindrical ornaments used for gilding.
Running Title.—The title of the work placed at the head of each page, above the text.

Section.—See Beating.
Set-off.—When the ink, not being properly dry, is transferred in beating and pressing to the page opposite.
Setting the Headband.—Is to form the leather at the head and tail of the book into a cap, to cover the headband.
Sewer.—The person who sews the sheets of a book together on the sewing press. Like folding, this is an operation generally performed by females.
Signature.—The capital letters or figures under the footline of the first page of each sheet, to indicate the order in which they should be placed.

Size.—Substances composed of gums, vellum, &c., used by the marbler and gilder.

Squares.—That portion of the boards of a volume which projects over the edges.

Start.—When any of the leaves, after binding, spring from the back and project from the general line of the edge, they are said to start.

Stitcher.—The party who sews together the sheets of a pamphlet or other work, which is covered with paper only.

Super-extra.—A book beat and forwarded in the best manner, having superior coloured end-papers, double headbands, and broad registers; rolled inside and double rolled outside with narrow rolls, or one broad roll.

Table.—The smooth side of the laying press.

Tail.—The bottom of the book.

Tools.—The name given to the brass ornaments used in gilding.

Turning up.—An operation of flattening the back previous to putting the book in the press to cut the fore-edge, whereby a groove is formed on the edge, when the back resumes its circular form.

Tying up.—The tying of a volume, after covering between two boards with strong cord, to mark the position of the bands, and to cause the leather to adhere to the sides of them.

Warp.—A process after the volume is finished, to give the boards a convex form, which tends to keep close the fore-edge of the book.

Waste.—The overplus sheets of a work after all the copies have been made up by the gatherer, and from which the binder is supplied with any imperfections.

Wrinkle—The uneven places in a book formed from being badly beaten or pressed.

INDEX.

THE END.

Londo : Printed by G. H. Davidson,
Tudor Street, New Bridge Street.

For EU product safety concerns, contact us at Calle de José Abascal, 56–1°,
28003 Madrid, Spain or eugpsr@cambridge.org.